It's *Never* Too Late

MAKE THE NEXT ACT OF YOUR LIFE
THE BEST ACT OF YOUR LIFE

Kathie Lee Gifford

W PUBLISHING GROUP

AN IMPRINT OF THOMAS NELSON

Published in Nashville, Tennessee, by W Publishing Group, an imprint of Thomas Nelson.

Thomas Nelson titles may be purchased in bulk for educational, business, fundraising, or sales promotional use. For information, please email SpecialMarkets@ThomasNelson.com.

Unless otherwise noted, Scripture quotations are taken from the Holy Bible, New International Version®, NIV®. Copyright © 1973, 1978, 1984, 2011 by Biblica, Inc.® Used by permission of Zondervan. All rights reserved worldwide. www.zondervan. com. The "NIV" and "New International Version" are trademarks registered in the United States Patent and Trademark Office by Biblica, Inc.®

Scripture quotations marked NASB are from the New American Standard Bible® (NASB). Copyright © 1960, 1962, 1963, 1968, 1971, 1972, 1973, 1975, 1977, 1995 by The Lockman Foundation. Used by permission. www.Lockman.org.

Scripture quotations marked LEB are from the Lexham English Bible. Copyright 2012 Logos Bible Software. Lexham is a registered trademark of Logos Bible Software.

Scripture quotations marked RGT are from the Revised Geneva Translation. Copyright © 2019 by Five Talents Audio. All rights reserved.

Any internet addresses, phone numbers, or company or product information printed in this book are offered as a resource and are not intended in any way to be or to imply an endorsement by Thomas Nelson, nor does Thomas Nelson vouch for the existence, content, or services of these sites, phone numbers, companies, or products beyond the life of this book.

ISBN 978-0-7852-3667-2 (eBook)
ISBN 978-0-7852-4121-8 (ITPE)
ISBN 978-0-7852-4900-9 (B&N signed edition)

Library of Congress Control Number: 2020943243

ISBN 978-0-7852-3664-1

Printed and bound by CPI Group (UK) Ltd, Croydon CR0 4YY

20 21 22 23 24 CPI 10 9 8 7 6 5 4 3

It's
Never
Too
Late

*With gratitude to my parents, Joanie and Eppie, who said they
loved me too much to deny me the privilege of making mistakes.*

*And for every mistake I've made (and there were many),
I thank my Lord and Savior, Jesus, Yeshua, for forgiving me.*

I Need to Make a Change in My Life

by Kathie Lee Gifford

I need to make a change in my life
To rearrange what's left of the rest of my life
I've been living far too long in this dusty old room
I need to plant a dream . . . I need to watch it bloom

I need to make a choice in my life
Surrender to the voice I've ignored all my life
I've been waiting far too long watching dreams pass me by
I need to learn to live before I die

I hunger to taste more while I still have the gift of time
To taste a wine so sweet, I never dreamed it could be mine
To savor every sunset and to say at the end of the ride
I smiled at ev'ry sunrise, I sailed on ev'ry tide
No question was unasked, no glance was ignored
I drank deep from the well, more than I could afford
I can't waste another chance, can't waste another day
Watching all my dreams just waste away

No regrets
No what-ifs
No if onlys
No what might have beens
I need to make a change in my life

Contents

CONTENTS

Foreword

What can I say about dreams? There's lots to be said about them. Everybody has them. Everybody wants them to come true.

It's always been my belief that you never get too old to dream. I often say (and mean it) that I wake up with a new dream every day . . . well, at least one, usually more. Dreaming is easy. Making them come true is the hard part.

A wish and a dream are not the same. You can sit around and wish all day long about wanting this and wanting that. But that's not gonna get you anywhere if you don't dream up a plan and then act on it.

I've often been quoted as saying, "In order to make dreams come true, you have to put legs, arms, feet, hands, and wings on them." In other words, you have to work your ever-lovin' butt off to get the job done. Of course, you also have to have a plan and a talent in whatever field that you want to be successful in. But with blood, sweat, and tears, it can be achieved. Most people are not willing to sacrifice sweat and tears, much less blood. Even though that's very graphic, it does amount to that.

Some are luckier than most and don't have as hard of a time achieving their goals, but it still takes time and devotion. I know it looks easy for people like me and Kathie Lee to say all of this, seeing as how we're both successful women. But believe me, we didn't get there without all of the things that I just talked about. We both paid our dues, we dreamed big, we paid big, and we're still doing it at our age.

I've always loved Kathie Lee, and I respect and admire her openness, her talent, her beauty, and her willingness to share her life with others. I know she has been an inspiration to me as well as millions of others through the years. I was fascinated, but not surprised, when she decided to leave a well-established, secure career to start a whole new chapter in her life.

It's Never Too Late is great and will be such an inspiration, not only for the older generation but to young ones as well. After all, a dream is a dream, and it can come true at any age. I've written books about dreaming and I've read many books on the subject, but this one covers it all and more. And just when I thought I knew everything there was to know about dreams. You go, girl! I will always love you and be dreaming along beside you.

—Dolly Parton
August 2020

Dream with Me

I never intended to take this stroll down memory lane. What began as a book that would help us all remember "we're not done yet" turned into a lot of looking back. But isn't that the way it goes? God always seems to have His own idea of what's best.

As I was writing, I realized the importance of knowing not only where you are but also where you've been and what got you there. That perspective can help you figure out where you want to go next.

So where *do* you want to go?

You might say, "Good question, Kathie Lee. I'm not sure" or "I haven't really thought about it" or "How the heck am I supposed to know that?"

I have one word for you: dream! Let me say it one more time to be sure you got it . . . *dream*.

If you're my age, or getting close, it's probably been a long time since you last thought back to those days when you had dreams of what or who you wanted to be when you "grew up."

But it's time, friend. It's time to ask yourself, "What would I do if I could?" Toss out the phrases *I can't* and *I don't know how* and start dreaming about the what-if that might get you off that couch and back into something you want to do.

Maybe me sharing my story will give you some perspective and help you get started on your own. At the heart of my personal dream of singing and being in movies is my love of inspiring and entertaining others, so hopefully, some of my stories will do just that for you.

Are you ready?

Dream with me. Because it's never too late to dream.

one

Begin Again

How do I begin to begin again?
Breathe deep and let all the fresh clean air in?
How do I find the courage to say
I'm gonna start a brand-new life today?

—"NEW EVERYTHINGS" BY KATHIE LEE
GIFFORD AND BRETT JAMES

Certain moments in life can take on a rich significance in retrospect. Take, for instance, the time I was kicked out of the Brownies. No, I'm not kidding. I actually was kicked out of the Brownies. They insisted I turn my beanie in. All because I had bought into the Join the Brownies, See the World propaganda.

I arrived at the first meeting super excited, but all I could see was the back of the beanie on the girl in front of me—who had bought into the same propaganda.

It turns out talking about the world is not the same as seeing the world.

For the first time in my young life I felt duped, disappointed

1

that what I'd been told was not actually true. So, I started my own Brownie troop at home, and the organization took umbrage and asked me to never show up again. (I think I remember my parents giggling, but I'm not sure.) That experience has stayed with me for decades.

Disappointment can do a number on you, but only if you let it. I'm not sure where I got the drive and determination to keep moving forward, even at the ripe old age of seven, but it likely had a lot to do with my dad and mom.

I was born into a wonderful family with two parents who knew very early on that they had an unusual child in me. They always showed their love in spite of my uniqueness, encouraging my adventures, circuses, concerts, and plays in the backyard. They let me raid the family pantry to open a corner store on our street. They smiled as I started the children's newspaper for our neighborhood. I'm eternally grateful to God for my parents.

I tried to foster the same kind of love and support in raising my own children, Cody and Cassidy. You'd have to ask them if I succeeded. Actually, please don't. Let them write a book that can't hurt my feelings when I'm dead. Regardless, they have turned out to be remarkable, delightful, completely unique, and imaginative individuals who are doing exactly what they were created to do—create.

Cody is an extraordinary screenwriter and producer. And Cassidy is an accomplished film and television actress. They're fun. They're kind. And I don't resent them for my stretch marks at all. They were worth it.

Today, I find myself at a point in life where the labels that technically apply to me could actually define me, if I let them. I'm a widow. And I'm an empty nester. Please don't throw in senior citizen—I already know that too. I'm basically alone for the first time in my long life. That thought by itself could either terrify me or thrill me. I'm trying very hard to be thrilled. Growing older is not for the faint of heart, but I truly believe that this next season of my life has the potential to be the best season in a life that, to this point, has been jam-packed with amazing opportunities and great adventures.

So, what's next? After lunch, that is.

I don't know, and that's the point. I can make the rest of my life what I want it to be. I can fill it up with people and have a celebration, sit by the fire and write an oratorio, or sit alone and have a pathetic pity party. For the very first time, it's my choice to make.

I moved from Connecticut to Nashville after eleven years on NBC's *TODAY* show with Hoda Kotb. I could not wait to get settled in and begin a brand-new life. One thing I've always loved is songwriting, so it was a real joy to have the opportunity to collaborate with singer-songwriter Brett James. "New Everythings" is one of the songs we composed for a movie that I'd written for Craig Ferguson and me to shoot in Scotland. In the film the heroine, Annabelle, is widowed and sets out on an unusual adventure that takes her to Scotland, leaving her former life in Nantucket completely behind. She is childless, jobless, but not hopeless.

I loved playing Annabelle. She's a pure spirit, doing the very best she can to find whatever joy is still available to her, perhaps hidden deep somewhere in the Highlands. As of this writing we have finally found the right distributor for the movie. It has taken over two years, but for a long time it looked like it was never going to happen. That's the risk you take when you dare to not only dream but set out to make those dreams come true. Even if it kills you.

Some of my dreams have taken years to come true—like *Scandalous*, the Broadway musical that took thirteen years and fourteen million dollars to create, only to close after three weeks. Nothing I have ever dreamed has been easy. Nothing. Show business is brutal and has left many a carcass on the red carpet. I don't intend to be one of them.

As Stephen Sondheim once said to me, "You did the work."

Yes, I did, and I'm still doing it.

There is joy in the struggle of hard work, and there is profound pleasure in the sweat of it. I may have twenty years left in this life, or I may have twenty minutes. But I'm going to drink this life to the dregs while I can. Because it's never too late to begin again.

two

Share Your First Love

We had so many good times
Why do good times always have to end?
Stopped countin' all the days
Since we went our separate ways
Now you show up with your "Hey, girl, how you been?"
Not again.

—"NOT AGAIN" BY KATHIE LEE GIFFORD

Yancy Bailey Spencer III. Even now, after all these years, the sound and sight of his name moves me deeply. Yancy was my first love. Not a flirty, silly high school kind of love. I mean a true love . . . the kind that stays with you for the rest of your life.

Actually, truth be told, my daddy was my first love.

You can read most of my growing-up story in my 1992 memoir, *I Can't Believe I Said That*. The *Reader's Digest* version is that my dad was a navy man stationed in Paris, France, with his wife, my mom, and my three-and-a-half-year-old brother, David, when I was born at the American Hospital in Paris. I was their "love child"; my mother always said she actually fell in love with my daddy during their two years in that gorgeous country.

Shortly after my debut we moved back to the States, which is where my sister, Michele (Michie), was born. Not long after that we were transferred to Germany and then finally back to Annapolis, Maryland, for good.

I had many rich experiences growing up in a family that had a lot of love to go around. With a full scholarship, I ended up attending Oral Roberts University in Tulsa, Oklahoma, as a drama major with a minor in music. I was a semester shy of graduating with a degree in music performance when I left the university in the winter of 1975.

People have questioned why I left early. All I can say is that I knew there was something else I was supposed to do and somewhere else I was supposed to go. Even then I knew when it was time to leave something that, on the surface, seemed a very good thing.

I can't explain this phenomenon except to say that it's a gnawing in my spirit that won't go away. A restlessness about *what is* and a growing excitement about *what's to be*. It's the way the Holy Spirit leads me, gently whispering into my being until I finally acknowledge it and my heart says yes.

I knew I was supposed to move to Los Angeles, but I was waiting for specific direction. I am the worst waiter in the world. I hate not being able to take action, and yet I know God does some of His best work in me when I am in a holding pattern.

While I was praying and waiting for answers, I started writing a book. I was twenty-two years old, had barely lived, and had no right to think that (1) I had anything deep or revelatory to say and (2) anyone would be interested in what I had to say if I said it. Still, something in me wanted to put my life on paper and preserve my experiences during one of the most tumultuous eras of our time—the '60s, a decade marked by the Vietnam War, "make love, not war" mentality, and a cultural loss of respect for authority. Hippies abounded, and although I was drawn to their sense of freedom and expression, there was also something in me (thank God) that was frightened by how that kind of freedom could damage the soul and, with the rampant drug use, the body.

I've always hated drugs. My body doesn't respond well to them. In fact, I'm allergic to many pharmaceutical drugs, which is probably why I wasn't curious to try marijuana, and certainly not LSD or any of the other hallucinogens.

I was a happy girl. I loved Jesus and wanted to serve Him with a faithful heart. At that time someone like me was called a Jesus freak. (Actually, I'm still a Jesus freak.)

I knew that I was living in a defining moment in our history, and I wanted to encapsulate it in writing so that someday, if God blessed me with a daughter, she would know what her mother had experienced. I sat down to write, and for three weeks, I barely got up, writing in longhand what eventually became *The Quiet Riot*.

Page one, chapter one began with these words: *I was fifteen. He was nineteen and all the things first loves are made of. Tall and tanned so deep, no winter's pale approached him.*

I know, but cut me some slack, okay? I never thought it would get published. I met the aforementioned Yancy Bailey Spencer III on his nineteenth birthday, July 2, 1969, on the boardwalk in Rehoboth Beach, Delaware, where my family spent the summers running an inn.

He was already a renowned surfer from Pensacola, Florida, on the Gulf Coast. It was instant. That's all I can say. Bam! I took one look and my heart was his.

Love at first sight is a real thing. This love I fell into with Yancy would stay with me in a profound way for the rest of my life, but also his, which ended suddenly.

When I met Yancy he was not a Christian. None of his surfer buddies were, either, but my sister, Michie, and I always shared with them about Jesus. They all thought that Jesus was about as cool as they came—they were just not sure He was God.

Our situation was complicated due to the geography between us. By the time I was a senior in high school, Yancy had already been a professional surfer traveling all over the world participating in surfing competitions for several years. There were no cell phones then, so we rarely got to speak. It was a great surprise when one day he called me at my house in Maryland inviting me to visit him and his family after Christmas in Pensacola. We had talked about getting married after I graduated (I know, I know), and I couldn't wait for the holidays to arrive so I could get on a plane to be with him and meet his family.

Certain moments sear themselves in your memory—this was one of them.

After Yancy picked me up at the airport, he took me across the beautiful bridge on the way to Gulf Breeze, where he lived. He stopped the car on the other side, looked at me with his beautiful blue eyes, and said, "I'm so happy you came, Kathryn." (He is the only person in my life who ever called me by my real name.) "Seeing you has made me realize how much I love Pamela."

What?

It turned out that he had met a beautiful young woman named Pamela in the months before, and as often happens when you are young and impetuous, he would marry her a few months later.

I remember going home to Maryland after that weekend and banging my head over and over again against a door. Stupid for sure. But certainly an expression of the pain and the hopelessness I felt at the time.

Several years later Yancy called to tell me the wonderful news that he had come to faith in Jesus at Rock Church in Virginia Beach and realized the mistake he had made in marrying so hastily. On a trip home to visit my family I met him on the boardwalk one night to cry and pray that God would show us a way to be together, but in the end we both believed that divorce was wrong and he should try and stay in the loveless, Christless marriage. His wife ultimately left him, but by then I had married my first husband, so we had missed our window of opportunity to be together.

Yancy went on to marry a beautiful Christian woman named Lydia who had, ironically, learned about him through reading my book *The Quiet Riot* (which had miraculously been published in 1976 and was a surprise bestseller).

Many years later, Lydia and their gorgeous eighteen-year-old daughter, Abigail, came to the studio to watch *Live with Regis and Kathie Lee*. Yancy had called and asked me if they could come to a taping while they were visiting New York looking at schools. Abigail was a gifted singer, dancer, and actress who wanted to pursue a career in the arts. I'll never forget the first time I met her. *Breathtaking* was the only word that came to mind.

During the show I acknowledged them in the audience and then invited them to visit with me in my dressing room afterward. While there, I called the head of casting at ABC, who just happened to have watched the show that morning.

"Send her over," she said to me. "I want to meet her."

That's how capricious this business is. One minute you're an unknown entity sitting in a television audience, a few hours later you're auditioning for *All My Children*, and nine months later you're accepting a *Soap Opera Digest* award for Outstanding Female Newcomer.

Abby lived at our house in Connecticut for the first six months after her move to New York to work on the soap opera. We all adored her. This extraordinary actress has since gone on to act in film and television hits such as *Mad Men*, *Suits*, and *Timeless*.

On the morning of February 14, 2011, Valentine's Day, I answered my dressing-room phone. It was Abby calling to tell me that Yancy had died while surfing in Malibu, California. He'd had a heart attack. He was sixty years old.

"Kathie," Abby cried, "will you please tell the world that my daddy is gone?"

I was incredulous.

"But, Abby . . ."

"My mom also wants you to. My whole family does." She paused. "Tell them that he loved Jesus and died exactly the way he would have wanted to."

So I did.

It was only later that I learned that Yancy had led dozens of young surfers to faith in Jesus. There is a statue of him on Pensacola Beach.

Who in your past has been important to you? If that person is still living, I urge you to reach out. For me, all I can do is say, "Rest in peace, sweet surfer, sweet friend. You will forever be my very first love."

three

Never Give Up

Lord, You have told me that if I have a need
I should just ask it of You.
There is never too great a task for You.
So, Lord, now I'm asking You.

—"ALL THAT I NEED" BY KATHIE LEE GIFFORD

With time and distance, and hopefully a dash of wisdom along the way, you're able to see everything that has happened in your life with a new perspective. In your recollections of the past, a pattern emerges, and a distinct path forward eventually becomes visible.

When I left Oral Roberts University in 1975 to move to Los Angeles, I decided to give myself one year to make it in a business that I had already been warned was brutal. I found a tiny, cheap rental apartment and got a C-list agent to begin making the rounds. To say I was green would be like saying that spring comes after winter. Even with years of performance experience behind me, I was woefully ill-prepared for the critical beating you receive when you audition for commercials, film, television, or even industrial shows.

I felt like a raw piece of meat during each interview. Then came the inevitable, endless wait by the phone for the call from your agent telling you that you didn't get the job.

I tried to convince myself it was all part of the learning process and that I would get better with each audition. But after six months, discouragement set in, which negatively affected my auditions. It was a perpetual Catch-22. My self-talk turned toxic.

You can do this, Kathie.

No, you can't, or you would have done it by now.

You're making a fool of yourself.

Your agent is going to dump you if you don't book a job.

Your money is running out, and so is the clock on the year you gave yourself.

Loser.

I paid the bills by appearing as an atmosphere person—essentially an "extra"—on *Days of Our Lives* and as the singer on Kathryn Kuhlman's television program *I Believe in Miracles*.

Kathryn Kuhlman was a well-known and controversial faith healer at the time who had quite the following. She was unusually eccentric and a little frightening to me. I had to audition for her, and I chose to sing "What a Friend We Have in Jesus," "How Great Thou Art," and "Amazing Grace," while she silently bore a hole into me with her steely eyes. After I finished, I held my breath. Kathryn Kuhlman glided over to me in her satin gown, took my face in her hands, pulled me close, and declared, "It's adorable."

I sang on her show every Sunday for the whole year, and I don't remember her saying one more word to me. The gig paid the bills, but it certainly wasn't taking me any closer to my mission of making it as a legitimate talent in Hollywood.

About nine months into my first year in Hollywood I began to get a little notice in the commercial world. I was getting callbacks, meaning casting agents would call my agent to schedule me for a second audition. This happened over and over for a few months. The same people were often in the waiting rooms with me, yet it seemed the jobs always went to actress Nancy Morgan. I wished to know her secret. What magic did she have that I lacked?

I frequently wanted to give up, go home, and become a florist or something else less stressful. Then I'd get a fresh burst of courage and yell out loud to myself, "Come on, Judy [a la Garland], *let's put on a show!*"

Despite my attempts to stay optimistic, I cried myself to sleep many a night, pleading with the Lord to break through for me. Finally, I had to get a real job, so I began working as a hostess at the El Torito Mexican restaurant on Ventura Boulevard in a neighborhood outside of Los Angeles. Honest work, of course, but depressing.

Then someone told me about a job in Vegas that had just opened up. One of the singers in a group called the Windsong Trio had dropped out of a show that was scheduled to open at the Landmark Hotel. The producers were frantic to find someone who could learn the show immediately and open in forty-eight hours. I never stopped to think how impossible that was. I was young and ignorant and desperate to actually work doing what I had longed to do my whole life.

I took the job, learned the show, and performed three times a day for the longest month of my twenty-two years on this planet. I was miserable. I was sharing a room with the other two Windsong singers: a Baptist preacher's daughter and an ex–beauty queen. They were both nice enough, but the craziness began each night after the third show. I'd head to bed, exhausted, and the two girls would head out for a fun-filled night of God knows what. Then I'd get up at about five in the morning just as they were returning. I admired their stamina but remember feeling deeply saddened that they were partying night after night.

This show finally came to a blessed end, and I returned to LA to continue auditioning for work. I was one week away from my self-imposed deadline of one year to "make it" when I auditioned for six new commercials. As per usual, perfect Nancy Morgan was at each audition, probably already counting her residuals.

To my utter astonishment I was chosen for five of the six commercials, but due to scheduling conflicts, I could only book three of them. I cried into the phone when I called my parents to tell them that I was actually, *finally*, on my way to a real career.

I shot the commercials one after the other and took great pleasure in smiling at Nancy Morgan, who was also cast, during each one. She smiled right back, as if to welcome me into the inner sanctum. It felt good. Commercials paid my bills, but they didn't really build my career. I needed to break into a series of some sort where I could gain stability in this crazy, completely unpredictable industry.

I tried out for a children's show and was convinced I nailed it. The head writer kept smiling at me and nodding his approval, but once again my agent had to deliver the news that I hadn't gotten the job. Not even a callback.

It seemed I was in the wrong business. I thought, *If I'm not right for a simple children's show, what am I ever going to be right for?*

My agent called one day soon after to say, "Kath, they want to see you for a new game show over at Ralph Edwards Productions. Have three songs ready."

"Okay," I agreed, wearily. *Here we go again.*

When I arrived at the audition, I thought someone had made a mistake. There was no one else waiting with me. I double-checked the address and time I had written down. Yes, I was in the right place, right on time. Suddenly a young woman appeared.

"Kathie Epstein?" she said.

"Yes," I answered. "Where is everybody?"

"It's just you," she replied. "Mr. Edwards will see you now."

I followed her into a large conference room full of people I'd never seen before. Except for one: the head writer of the children's show that I'd thought for sure I was going to get a month before. His name was Gary Bloom, and he smiled a big smile and winked at me.

What is going on? I wondered.

All I could do was launch into the songs I'd prepared. I had barely finished the last one when the legendary producer Ralph Edwards walked over to me to shake my hand.

"Welcome to Ralph Edwards Productions." He smiled graciously. "Welcome to *Name That Tune*."

I was stunned. In an instant, my entire life changed. The trajectory of my career went through the roof and nothing would ever be the same. That's showbiz.

As it turned out, Gary Bloom had told my agent that while he had loved my earlier audition, he thought I was too sophisticated for the children's show. But he was working on another show that he was sure I'd be perfect for.

He was right. I learned two hundred songs in five days and shot the shows for the entire year in a few weeks.

We taped at the NBC Studios in Burbank right next to *The Tonight Show*, and, finally, I thought, *So this is what it's like to make a living doing what you love to do.*

As I walked through the gate for the first time with my agent and parents, past the security guard who greeted me warmly, I whispered this prayer: "Dear Jesus, I know my life is about to change. Thank You, Lord, for this amazing new chapter in my life. Please help me to treat every single person I meet exactly the same—from the executive producers to the guard at the gate. And I will give You all the praise."

I squeezed my daddy's hand. He was still smiling because the guard had confused him with one of his all-time heroes, Roy Rogers.

"Hi, Roy," he had said to him. "Welcome back."

"Thank you, kindly," my daddy had responded, never letting on. We giggled.

A few weeks later we wrapped the season, and I headed to the car in the parking lot feeling elated. It had gone well. I hadn't made one mistake in two hundred songs. I was on my way. My daddy came up after me, and the same security guard stopped him.

"Mr. Epstein," he said, "I just want you to know that every time your daughter came through the gate, love came with her."

"Thank you, kindly," my daddy answered with tears in his eyes.

Thank You, Jesus, for the reminder that it's never too late to *never give up.*

four

Tell the Truth

For some crazy reason I was thinking last night
Of a marriage gone wrong long ago
And the years I spent married to "Mr. Right"
It's funny how memories flow.

—"MR. RIGHT" BY KATHIE LEE GIFFORD

I have written very little about my first marriage and spoken publicly about it even less. The truth is, it was only a marriage in the pages of the law. I had a legal relationship with Paul Johnson, a brilliant composer, from April 23, 1976, to spring of 1983. Though Paul and I were married, we shared only one thing—our faith.

We met in 1973 while I was a student at Oral Roberts University and a member of the World Action Singers, a group that performed on ORU's weekly telecast. Paul was a friend of university founder Oral Roberts's son, Richard, and came by the studio in Hollywood while we were recording. When I moved to LA a year later, I attended two Bible studies—one at Pat and Shirley Boone's house in Beverly Hills and another at Paul's house in Woodland Hills, out in the San

Fernando Valley. That is where I had found an apartment and where I also started attending services at Church on the Way in Van Nuys. I was deeply affected by the teaching of Pastor Jack Hayford, the minister who had founded it.

Pastor Jack was truly a godly man and one of the few people anywhere who believed that young Christian women and men could be called into the arts—even to successful careers in show business. I consider him to be one of my dearest friends to this day because he believed God's calling on my life and encouraged it. He also knew Paul but nothing of our marital problems.

I was a virgin on my wedding night with Paul, and still considered myself one when he left me five years later. It's hard even now to explain why I stayed so long in a sexless marriage. I certainly would never do it again. But back then divorce had much more of a stigma, and no one in my family was divorced. I believed that God could heal our marriage and prayed every day that He would.

Within a year of our wedding day I moved into our guest room and stayed there until our marriage was over. During those years I experienced the deepest loneliness of my life. I felt disgraced, rejected, and worst of all, like a failure at something I had hoped to be—a loving wife.

Before we married, Paul told me that he was a virgin too. We talked about how we wanted to honor God's Word and present ourselves as a gift to the person we would eventually marry. But after we were married he wanted nothing to do with me. Nothing.

We put on a good, faithful face for the world we lived in, the contemporary–Christian music world, which was growing wildly in the '70s in California. But in private we were both desperately unhappy.

At one point we attempted counseling. We met with James Dobson, the founder of Focus on the Family, but it was a disaster.

Dr. Dobson believed that I was the problem and that I should give up my career to attend to Paul's ambition and talent and keep his home neat and organized. Paul immediately responded, "No way! I don't want her waiting around at home for me. I *want* her to work." We sat in silence during the two-hour road trip home, no closer to any sort of breakthrough in our marital issues.

Though we had shared the same bed, we had never been truly intimate, and now we'd stopped talking too. He would work in the studio until the wee hours of the morning or compose all night in the living room. Occasionally he'd go out on the road as musical director for Debby Boone. I'd been making a name for myself on two different television game and variety programs, *Name That Tune* and *Hee Haw Honeys*, and was doing tons of commercials. The only time I was joyful was when I could escape the despair of my marriage and lose myself in my work. I was grateful to have something to distract me.

One day I came home from a three-week run on the road with Bill Cosby—a two-year stint where I was his opening musical act on his tour as a comedian. The lock on our front door had broken just prior to my leaving on the trip, and apparently Paul hadn't fixed it as he said he would because when I tried to go in the house, the door simply flew open.

I walked into our living room and found it completely trashed. My first thought was, *Oh my God, we've been robbed!* Then I noticed that the piano was missing, and it dawned on me, *No, he's left me.*

I had had no warning. There had been no discussion of a separation. Nothing.

In the kitchen I found a short note on the counter that said, "Maybe now you'll know that I mean it," with a phone number in case of emergency. To this day I have no idea what he meant.

Nothing in my young life had prepared me for such a shock.

It's amazing how survivor mode kicks in almost immediately. I had to clean up the mess. I've never functioned well among chaos; I've always loved a nice, clean, organized environment around me, so I got to work. I went to the closet to get our vacuum cleaner, but he had also taken it, so I said to myself, "Fine. I'll go buy a new one." And I did.

I brought the new vacuum cleaner home and opened the box only to discover it needed to be assembled. I'm not very handy in that way, but I was sure he hadn't taken the toolbox because he was even worse than I was at such things. It took forever, but I'll never forget the sound of that vacuum when I turned it on and it began to suck up all the ugliness in that room.

I vacuumed for hours. I moved furniture, washed all the dirty dishes, and unpacked my laundry from my trip. I metaphorically and literally cleaned house.

Today I remember this as one of the most deeply important moments in my life, when God met me at the point of my brokenness and said, "It's okay, Kathie. We can fix this. He didn't love you, but I do."

Tears streamed down my face all that day, but they were cleansing tears. I fell asleep in the guest room where I'd slept for years. I didn't miss him at all. There wasn't anything to miss. We both knew it was a whole new world now.

I called my family and told them the truth. I also called Sam Haskell, my trusted friend and agent. I had met Sam when he was working in the mail room at the William Morris Agency. We became fast friends. He said to me, "One day I'm going to be an agent and you're going to be my very first client." And that's exactly what happened in 1980. He became, and still is to this day, my closest male friend.

Soon after Paul left, Sam called to tell me I'd been asked to cohost the number-one morning show in LA. Regis Philbin had suddenly left for a national show with Mary Hart, and the producers were desperate to save the show after his departure. I was scheduled to fly to Atlanta to join Cosby for the weekend, but Sam and I both agreed that to cohost for a day would be a good break from the mess I'd been cleaning up.

It went so well the producers asked me to stay for the week. And then come back for the next one, which, of course, I couldn't do. But I had a blast cohosting the show and getting out of my comfort zone.

I never dreamed that those few short appearances would change my life forever. A few weeks later Sam called to tell me that the executive producer of *Good Morning America* was flying in to meet me and discuss the possibility of my moving to New York to be a part of the show.

"What do they want me to do?" I remember asking. "I'm not a journalist."

"That's what they like about you. They think you might be able to fill Joan Lunden's position whenever she decides to retire."

"What!" I shrieked. "Joan Lunden, the cohost?"

Sam tried to calm me down. "They want to start grooming someone to succeed her. A fresh face, and they like the fact that you're just yourself on the air. You don't *interview* people; you just talk to them. And you're funny and unpredictable. The producer's coming in next week."

Well, she did, and we met, and in time I moved to New York City, where I was living when my divorce became final.

I saw Paul Johnson just one more time. In 2011 my musical *Saving Aimee*, which was ultimately named *Scandalous* when we got to Broadway, was having a run in Seattle, Paul's hometown. The morning of our two closing performances, my sister, Michie, called to tell me that Paul had bought a ticket to the matinee and wanted to know if he could say hello. (Paul had stayed in touch with Michie over the years. His father, who was an abdominal surgeon, had once saved her life, so it wasn't unusual for them to occasionally communicate.)

Seeing Paul was the last thing in the world I needed or wanted that day. I was exhausted. But I had forgiven Paul years before and had prayed often for him since our marriage ended, so I called him and invited him to join me for lunch. He attended the matinee, loved the show, and asked if he could see it again that night. Afterward he joined me again, this time for dinner. He never said a word about why he left me the way he did or why he married me in the first place, and I didn't ask. I hugged him good night and wished him a happy life.

I still do.

Ironically, soon after I moved to the Nashville area, I was leaving Mojo's Tacos (a favorite restaurant) when a man who was with his wife stopped me and said, "Hi, I just want you to know that your first husband saved our marriage." His wife nodded in agreement.

I said, "I'm sorry, what?"

"Yes, we were on the verge of divorce and we went to see him. You know he's a marriage and relationship counselor now, right?"

I said, "No, I didn't know that, but I'm so happy he could save your marriage. He sure couldn't save ours!"

You've got to love God's sense of humor.

Sometimes opening up to the truth of a situation isn't as much about setting the record straight as it is about setting yourself straight in light of that truth. It's never too late to tell the truth— even if it's only to yourself.

five
Redeem What Goes On
Behind Closed Doors

Create in me a clean heart, Oh Lord
And renew a right spirit within me.
Wash me afresh and bathe me anew.
Make me more like You and
Help me to do what You want me to do.
O give me a fresh cup of mercy.

—"A FRESH CUP OF MERCY" BY KATHIE LEE GIFFORD

After *Name That Tune* my career exploded. I spent a year in Nashville shooting the sitcom *Hee Haw Honeys*, was doing commercials, and opened for all the top comics in show business—including Bill Cosby. Okay, I know what you're wondering.

Bill was always gracious and generous to me and my backup singers—my sister, Michie, and Denise Carley, my high school friend. Often, after we arrived at whatever hotel we were working at—let's say Harrah's in Lake Tahoe—and checked into our rooms, Bill would call and ask, "Why don't you all just come over to the house and stay with me? We'll play tennis and the chef will make you anything you want." We always agreed and never had a moment's hesitation.

While we were onstage opening for Bill, he would be busy in his dressing room making us cappuccinos that he'd offer us as we came offstage. Then he'd quickly take the stage himself to perform his always brilliant comedy routine.

I witnessed a constant parade of people coming and going into his dressing room: his mother and her entourage of friends, along with all manner of different members of society. I never knew what took place as it was truly none of my business.

The only time I had an unusual encounter with Bill was the last time I flew with him in his plane from California to New York in the fall of 1981. I was scheduled to meet the producers of *Good Morning America* to do a camera test for them. This would determine if they did, indeed, want to hire me for the program. Bill offered to fly me there on his plane.

"Come on down to the house in the Palisades the night before. We'll have a little dinner and get an early start for New York before all the traffic."

"Sounds good, Bill, thank you."

After two years performing and traveling with this man, I had not an ounce of trepidation going to his home for the night. He greeted me warmly as he always did. He showed me to my room. And then he joined me for dinner an hour later. Finally, he walked me back to my room to say good night. There, outside my door, he did something he had never done before.

He took my face in his hands, and he kissed me.

I was stunned, but I didn't feel panicked.

"Bill!" I said, firmly pushing him away. "We're friends. You don't want to do this."

"Okay," he said jovially and kissed me on the top of my head. "Good night."

And he disappeared down the hallway. That was it.

I was as surprised as the rest of the world when, years later, Bill Cosby, at one time the most respected and admired man in America, was accused of all manner of despicable acts with a myriad of women. I asked Michie and Denise, "Am I crazy? Did he ever try anything with you?"

They both assured me he had not. He had never been anything other than a gentleman to them.

It wasn't the only time in my career when my personal experience with a celebrity—for better or worse—differed drastically from details published in the media. On another trip, around the same time I worked with Bill Cosby, I was in Jupiter, Florida, scheduled to be a guest on the popular *Dinah Shore Show*. Dinah was dating Burt Reynolds at the time, and the plan was to tape a week's worth of shows from Burt's dinner theater. The producers had also booked the composer Paul Williams, actors Lee Majors and James Brolin, and the Gatlin Brothers—Larry, Rudy, and Steve—for the whole week.

The idea was to have Dinah surrounded by men who adored her, and they all did. Everyone adored Dinah Shore. She was America's sweetheart at the time. The problem was that Dinah's longtime manager, the legendary Henry Jaffe, had not signed another client in decades, until he suddenly signed a relatively unknown young singer/actress—me. And he had booked me to come on the show and announce that I was the new face of Diet Coke—a huge break for me and one that would put me on the map of corporate sponsorship. My parents flew in, the executives from Coca-Cola flew in, and I showed up at the studio filled with gratitude that all this amazing opportunity was coming my way.

I had met the Gatlin Brothers in Nashville on the set of *Hee Haw Honeys*, so I was delighted to see some familiar faces. The rest of the gentlemen I didn't know, but they were all very sweet and congratulatory to me.

I was excited as I stood in the wings, all wired up and ready to make my entrance near the end of the first show. But Dinah never announced me. She completely ignored the producers, the director, and the stage manager frantically signaling for her to do so.

The show ended, and I stood there, stunned. What could have happened? Was it just a technical mistake? My manager assured me that the next day's show would be different. Dinah had been confused—this time it would all go as planned.

But it didn't. The exact same thing happened, and I was completely mortified. Though I remained stoic, I wanted to get on the next plane out of Florida and cry my eyes out from the humiliation.

Finally, the producers assured me that they had convinced Dinah she couldn't do this again. She agreed to introduce me on the third day of shooting. I couldn't stay in my hotel room and feel sorry for myself. My family was there, and all the execs from Coca-Cola had agreed to stay as well.

That night we went to a local restaurant for dinner, and when my parents and I arrived, every diner in the place stood up and started applauding. I looked at the sweet faces and realized my audience was the staff and crew of the *Dinah Shore Show*. They wanted to offer their support after my three days of embarrassment.

I had dealt with the cruelty of what Dinah did in ignoring, even snubbing, me on her show and pretended I was just fine with all the delays. But, ironically, the kindness of these wonderful people who had watched it happen sent me flying into the ladies' room to sob my eyes out. I was grateful for each and every one of them.

The next day the show went off without a hitch. Dinah introduced me with her sugary southern drawl. I sang a Barry Manilow song and sat down with the other guests for the interview. Dinah made all kinds of lovely, flattering compliments and maintained a fake smile.

Soon enough it was over, and I could finally have this painful experience in the rearview mirror of my career. The whole thing had been surreal, and I made a mental note that no matter what happened—no matter how successful I would be blessed to become—I would never treat another person so disrespectfully or cruelly.

After the taping we all met up in the hotel lobby. Larry Gatlin and I had agreed earlier to spend some time together. So when everyone showed up except Larry, I asked his brother Rudy, "Where's Larry? We were gonna meet here."

Rudy looked at me nervously and said, "Uh, he must still be up in the room. Why don't you go check on him?"

"All right," I said. "What's the room number?"

Rudy told me, and I went up the elevator in search of the correct room. I knocked on the door and heard what sounded like Larry's voice.

"Wait a minute . . . let me get a towel," he said, kind of frantically. Suddenly the door flew open and there, indeed, was Larry wrapped in a towel, the darkened room behind him.

"Come on in, Kat," he said as he opened the door. He looked a mess. I was thinking something wasn't quite right, but surely he would find the light switch at any moment, get cleaned up, and go downstairs with me to join our group.

Instead he began talking feverishly. "Got to get to my plane . . . they've got the engines running, gotta get to my . . . gotta get . . ."

"Get what, Larry? What's wrong?" I said, noticing now that he was sweating profusely and shaking badly.

I know nothing about drugs. *Nothing.* But it was obvious that Larry was on way too much of something, and I had no idea how to help him.

"Larry, what can I do?" I asked, somewhat desperately. "Should I call someone to come? Should I call Rudy and Steve?"

"No, no, no," he insisted. "Let me just get in bed for a little while and calm down. I'll be fine. Let me lay down for a minute."

"Okay," I said and continued to stand there, concerned and confused.

His shaking became uncontrollable, and he was clearly scared. "Kat, please hold me. Please, Kat, I can't stop shaking."

I did not hesitate. I got on the bed with my friend and held him and held him and held him as he cried, whimpered, shook, and sweated until the sheets were wet.

Finally—I have no idea how many hours later—he fell asleep in my arms like a baby. I waited until I was sure he was okay, then stood up. I looked back at him sleeping peacefully.

"Oh, dear Jesus," I prayed, "please help my friend."

I left quietly, closing the door behind me.

Soon afterward Larry went to rehab, where he got the help he so desperately needed. He's been sober for decades and has continued his incredibly successful career.

Larry and I remained friends, but we never mentioned what had happened in Florida until one night at a Gatlin Brothers concert at Carnegie Hall in New York City. Frank and I were seated in the mezzanine when Larry suddenly said, "Ladies and gentlemen, I want you to look over there." He pointed to me. "See her? See her? That lady is my dear friend, Kathie Lee Gifford. For the first time I want to thank her publicly for saving my life a long, long, long time ago. She saved me from getting on a plane and going to get more drugs that likely would've killed me."

I sat there, uneasy at the attention, but so happy for my friend.

"Stand up, Kathie," Frank said.

"No, honey." I just waved back at Larry and blew him a kiss. There was no need to stand. That's what friends are for.

Redemption is available for everyone but is only effective when it's embraced. One day it *will* be too late. Until then, seek it out. It's there for the asking.

six

Remember How It Started

How do you measure a lifetime?
By the hours or the days or the years?
You measure the memory.
You treasure the moment.
You remember all the blessings you've been given
And thank the good Lord above
For every moment you've been loved,
Every hour, every day that you've been livin'.
That's how you measure a lifetime.

—"HOW DO YOU MEASURE A LIFETIME"
BY KATHIE LEE GIFFORD

I have always been fascinated to hear the stories of how people first met. A moment that seems insignificant sometimes turns into a momentous shift in one's destiny.

I had one such moment early in the summer of 1982. I had just moved to New York City to begin my year at *Good Morning America*. It was four in the morning, and I was preparing to tape an ALPO commercial with a stinky basset hound. How this assignment was going to help develop me into a world-class anchor of a major network's morning show, I had no idea, but there I was, walking down a hallway.

I passed a dressing room where a man, an on-air guest, was leaning over a sink, apparently putting in his contact lenses. What I noticed first, I have to be honest, was the physique of this mystery man. He had the single greatest set of buns I had ever seen.

I had recently undergone a procedure called radial keratotomy, which involved a doctor putting liquid cocaine on my cornea and proceeding to make small radial cuts with a razor blade. This was pre-LASIK, and it resulted in twenty-twenty vision for the first time in my life.

"Have I got an operation for you," I said to the unrecognizable man with his face in the sink.

"Yeah—with a fool on either end," he replied.

I just chuckled and continued on my way to the studio.

Later I learned that the magnificent "tight end" belonged to one of the most famous athletes/sportscasters in the world—Frank Gifford.

I don't actually recall our very first face-to-face meeting, but obviously when I did meet him I discovered that his face rivaled his gluteus maximus. Even at fifty-two years old he was matinee-idol handsome. And sweet and modest. We liked each other instantly, but I was twenty-nine and getting divorced and he was on his second marriage with three children and a grandchild.

From insider gossip at Good Morning America it was widely believed he was miserable in his marriage at the time, but Frank never spoke unkindly about his wife to me. He was elegant and classy and concerned for my well-being. He knew that journalism was a new frontier for me, as it had been for him a few years earlier, and he was always the first colleague to offer his advice and support. I was truly grateful to him.

On my birthday, August 16, I received a gift from someone—a bottle of champagne with a card that read, "Happy birthday to us, happy birthday to us, happy birthday dear Kathie Lee, happy birthday to us! Love, Frank."

I had no idea until then that we shared a birthday. But I soon learned from spending time with him that we also shared values, had similar senses of humor, and followed the same faith.

He was honest that he had fallen away from his Pentecostal beliefs years before and no longer went to church. But he still prayed and totally believed that Jesus was the Son of God. He was completely comfortable talking to me about my faith, which I welcomed in a new and different environment.

We began a beautiful friendship that deepened through the next four years as Frank experienced loss and tragedy and heartbreak in his personal life. Anytime he was facing a difficult situation he called me to see if he could take me to lunch or dinner. I felt privileged that he would seek my comfort and company.

I had started dating someone in 1984 who Frank didn't like at all for me. He didn't like the way this boyfriend treated me and kept asking why I stayed in such a roller-coaster relationship with a man who obviously didn't love me.

"Please tell me you're not going to marry him," he'd say.

"I might," I'd reply with a laugh. "It's none of your business."

Finally, after my boyfriend and I broke up for the ninth time in two years, Frank and I went for a walk, and he said to me, "You are going to hang out with me until you're over this guy." I walked away from him after he said this, but even after a block I could still feel him watching me, so I turned and looked back. Sure enough, he was still standing down the street, staring at me.

"I mean it, Kath," he yelled. "I'm not going to let you go back to him."

I was in a terrible romantic rut. The kind where one day you're euphoric and the next you're miserable. But I couldn't seem to find the strength to get out. Frank was determined to be the strength I needed, and he kept his word. His marriage to his second wife had deteriorated and was in the final stages of divorce. He was faithful to continue to be my friend and accompany me to whatever was going on in my life—whether it was personal or professional.

Finally, one day he called to see how I was doing. I asked, "Did you get the invitation for that dinner ABC is throwing for Walter Annenberg?"

"Yes," he answered.

"Are you going to take me?"

"I can't, Kath, I'm sorry. I'm leaving town for Palm Beach, then I'm headed to Santa Fe. I'll be gone about a week."

"Okay," I answered, "then I'll just go with some other tall, dark, and handsome guy."

He laughed. "I'll call you when I get back."

"Okay." I laughed, too, and hung up the phone.

Ten minutes later my phone rang again.

"Okay, I'll take you."

I smiled.

The night of the dinner he picked me up and gave me a small box. I couldn't imagine what was in it. I opened it to find the most beautiful Rolex watch with an unusual brown face.

"Why?" I looked at him.

"Because it's the color of your eyes."

That night we slow danced for the first time, and I experienced what it was like to actually be in his arms. I could sense all our colleagues' eyes on us—they were as surprised as I was with what seemed to be happening. Something changed in me that night, but it wasn't until weeks later that I finally knew what it was.

It was the summer of 1986, a year after I began cohosting the *Morning Show* with Regis Philbin. I had purchased a small house in the Hamptons and had just moved in over Memorial Day. Every Friday morning after the show ended, Frank would pick me up in his Jaguar and drive me out to the Hamptons for the weekend. We'd have lunch at my house and then he would drive to his attorney's home. He'd stay there until Sunday when he'd take me back to the city.

I couldn't wait for Fridays. I'd rush out of the studio and there he'd be. Like clockwork.

One weekend the US Open was being held at Shinnecock Hills Golf Club in Southampton. Frank and I had been invited to an opening night party at a beautiful home in Bridgehampton.

Just after arriving he said, "I'm gonna say hello to a few people. I'll see you in a bit. You okay?"

"Sure," I said. It wasn't as if we were dating, so I didn't expect him to hang out with me the whole night.

Ten minutes later he was suddenly next to me.

"Okay," he said, "I've done my duty, and now I've come home."

He never left my side the rest of that night.

The guests began to play with a device called the Music Box, a precursor to karaoke that allowed you to sing a famous song and record it onto a cassette tape, which you then got to keep. Frank and I chose "You Don't Bring Me Flowers." I started by singing the Barbra Streisand part, "You don't bring me flowers. You don't sing me love songs." And then Frank sang, "YouhardlytalktomeanymorewhenIcomethroughthedoor attheendoftheday."

I had never met anyone who could sing perfectly in tune yet was completely incapable of staying in rhythm. It was hysterical, and each time we sang the song it became increasingly more hysterical. He just couldn't for the life of him keep the beat.

At one point I fell off the sofa, crying with laughter. I just lay there and couldn't stop.

He was laughing, too, and as he reached down to lift me to my feet, I looked up at him and thought, *I never want to spend another day of my life without him in it.*

Frank asked me to marry him on August 10, 1986, in Atlantic City, where Regis and I were performing at the Trump Plaza. On Saturday, October 18, I became his wife in a small quiet ceremony on the beach in Bridgehampton at his attorney's house.

We only had one day together as Mr. and Mrs. Frank Gifford before he had to announce a Monday Night Football game at Giants Stadium. We raced off to Gurney's Inn in Montauk followed furiously by the paparazzi who had been hiding in the dunes trying to grab a shot of the ceremony. They failed.

It's always so sweet to remember back to how we met, became friends, and then joined together as man and wife. I'm sure there are people in your life that you have meet-cute stories about too. Take the time to remember them, even if they happened long ago. I know doing so will sweeten your day.

Frank Gifford was my husband for almost twenty-nine years. None of my memories of him have faded. I can even still smell him. I know I always will.

seven

Say I'm Done

Tender Savior, gracious Lord
How can I express
My grateful heart for all You do
How You love, how You lead, how You bless
Gentle Savior, loving Lord
How can I repay
The debt I owe for all You've done
Every moment, every hour, every day
Gentle
Gentle grace, gentle grace.

—"GENTLE GRACE" BY KATHIE LEE GIFFORD

In the mid-1970s I made a great deal of gospel music and performed all over the country, mostly in churches. Many of the people I met were wonderful, sincere, godly believers, but I didn't love the experience of it because too many of them weren't—namely some of the pastors. I witnessed a lot of greed, pride, lust, and ambition. It saddened me.

Even more than that, I knew deep down the church setting wasn't the arena God had designed for me. I was too much of an entertainer, too much rimshot, pratfall, and goofball. Too Lucy Ricardo, not enough Sandi Patty (although I loved them both).

I recorded an album in 1976 called *Friends* with my sister, Michie. It was received nicely. Because of that Michie and I started doing quite a few concerts, conventions, and television appearances.

One day Michie and I were singing together at a church in Eugene, Oregon. Michie's baby, Shannie, was three months old, but when Michie was pregnant, she had experienced horrendous gastric and intestinal problems. Months earlier she had called me into her bathroom to see (I apologize for this, but it's critical to the story) an example of what she was experiencing.

"Kath," she said sincerely and understandably concerned, "is this normal?"

I took one look at the blood and mucus, pus and fecal matter in the toilet. Even though I'd never been pregnant, I knew there was no way that was normal.

She saw five gastroenterologists after that and every one assured her she was fine; it was all part of the pregnancy process.

Back to our concert in Eugene. Michie completely collapsed after the service. We rushed her to Seattle, Washington, where my first husband's parents lived. Paul's father, a renowned abdomen surgeon, immediately placed Michie on the living room sofa and started an IV.

I took three-month-old Shannie and began the horrendous process of weening her off of her mother's milk. She cried hysterically for days.

My father-in-law admitted Michie into Swedish Medical Center, where they tried to stabilize her for the next few days. Doctors told us that, in the condition she was in, she would never survive surgery.

Dear God, it's hard to tell this story. I was up all night trying to get Shannie to take formula, then would go to the hospital and spend all day watching my beloved, emaciated sister lie in her hospital bed, hooked up to machines. A constant parade of doctors and nurses came in and out of her room.

She had acute ulcerative colitis. Hopelessness was the prevailing prognosis. She was seriously close to death, and I could barely look at her or her precious baby, who I feared would never know her amazing mother.

Finally, Paul's father believed she had gained enough strength to survive the operation. My mother and Michie's husband, Craig, flew in from Maryland. The doctors discovered that 80 percent of Michie's five-foot-long large intestine was destroyed, leaving 20 percent that had the consistency of wet tissue paper. It had to be removed and an ostomy bag had to be attached to her small intestine.

To our amazement, Michie survived the operation, and we all returned to the Johnson home for some desperately needed rest. In the middle of the night, my father-in-law received a call from the hospital: Michie had had a grand mal seizure and was barely holding on to life. She needed her mother and her husband, and she needed her sister to stay home and take care of her only child.

The hours agonizingly blurred one into another. Michie went on to have two more grand mal seizures. The doctor told Craig that it was time to say goodbye. He cried into our mother's arms, wailing, "God, Joanie, they've done such a number on her."

Then Michie fell into a coma, a coma none of us ever believed she would come out of.

Mom and Craig and I prayed. What else could we do? Meditate? Do a rain dance? Check our horoscopes? Cross our fingers?

No, our only other option was to wait. And waiting is excruciating (especially for me, the worst waiter in the world). I went to see

Michie in her room and sat down next to her bedside. I was furious with God. How could He allow such a thing to happen to this unbelievably faithful person?

It was during this time that Michie suddenly emerged from the coma. She looked at me and said, "Don't curse God for this bag, Kathie. It means I get to live the rest of my life."

As overjoyed as I was that she had survived the surgery and all the seizures, I was devastated that I had lost all faith that God could heal her. I was ashamed.

It took several years after returning to Maryland for Michie to recover. But she did. And then she began to share her amazing experience of God's grace with others.

Shannie, though tiny, began to grow and heal too. One year after she was born we were told that she had pulmonary stenosis—a heart defect that would have to be watched closely as the days went by. A year later, after no problems in her health, Shannie went in for her regular checkup, and her doctors told her parents that she needed emergency surgery.

Shannie turned two years old at the Children's Hospital in Washington, DC. We had a little party for her with the other precious children who were suffering from all manner of diseases. It broke my heart to see that so many of them were alone, with no one to suffer with them. They were wards of the state. Shannie was scheduled for surgery the day of her celebration.

"Juice, Mommy!" she said over and over again that morning. "Hungry, Mommy!" She wasn't allowed to eat or drink anything, and her surgery kept getting delayed. We did our best to divert her attention.

"Let's walk down the hall, Shannie Roo," I suggested, using the nickname I loved to call her. Shannie, as tiny as you can imagine a two-year-old could be, was prepped for surgery and wearing her miniature surgical gown. One of the indelible pictures seared into my mind is the image of her walking down the hall with her little bottom peeking out at me, dragging her carved turtle by a string. She had no idea what pain awaited her. No idea what trauma was about to be put on her beautiful baby body. No idea that she might have celebrated her last birthday.

Shannie was eventually put onto an adult gurney that was to be taken into surgery. Only Michie and Craig were allowed to accompany her to the elevator where they could kiss their beloved child goodbye. When the elevator doors closed, Michie watched her "I've got this" husband sob like a baby.

But here's the reality: the day Shannie survived her surgery, two of the children in her wing died. We cried both tears of joy and tears of sorrow. Life is never so hard as on days like that when some are blessed to keep the one they love and others have to let a loved one go, and none of it makes any human sense.

Michie and I had been booked to go to Charlotte, North Carolina, to appear on the *Praise the Lord* telecast just two months after Shannie's surgery. Obviously, I had informed the producers that it was a very difficult time for my sister. The last thing she wanted to do was leave her still-healing toddler to travel anywhere. But Michie was determined that God wanted her to tell her story of His faithfulness to her and her baby girl.

You see, there was a prevailing teaching at the time that sin caused all suffering and that God couldn't work miracles without first a confession of sin.

None of this was biblically true, so I told the producers that Michie and I would only appear on the show if we were allowed to sing three songs and allotted enough time for Michie to tell her testimony: that no, God didn't heal her instantly of her disease and no, He didn't heal Shannie instantly either, but He got them through both seasons of despair and never left their sides. He healed them through prayers and doctors and medicine. And that, too, was a miracle!

The producers agreed to our terms, and Michie and I traveled to Charlotte for the broadcast only to discover that the host, Jim Bakker, was out of town. He was at a convention in Florida, and his wife, Tammy Faye, would be hosting that day's telecast. *That's fine*, I thought, *as long as they comply with our understanding.*

The telecast began with no mention of Michie or me as guests. It went on and on until it was almost time to wrap. Finally, I couldn't stand it any longer. I went to the senior producer to express my frustration only to be told, "I'm sorry, but the Holy Spirit is moving."

I exploded, "Well, the Holy Spirit is moving me to leave this place right now if you don't honor the commitment you made to my sister!"

The senior producer looked at me, terrified. No one was used to this kind of reaction from me, but I didn't care. I knew Tammy Faye was insecure and jealous of every other woman and hated to give up the spotlight, even for a second. I'd also heard she was having marital problems. I was truly sorry for her, but you don't let those truths overwhelm the truth that you have made a promise. God expects you to keep promises just as He does.

We finally were called onstage and sang one song, but Michie never did get the chance to share her testimony. As the final seconds of the telecast were winding down, Tammy Faye pretended to care about my sister and her daughter, but when the light on the camera went from green to red, she walked away from her midsentence.

Something huge in me died that day. I determined I would never again take one penny for any Kingdom work. Never. And I haven't.

Only later I would learn that we had been in Charlotte on the very same day Jim Bakker admittedly had sex with a twenty-one-year-old girl named Jessica Hahn. Compassion washed all over me for Tammy Faye and for Jessica Hahn. I could relate to both women for different reasons.

It would be years before I reentered the gospel world with a CD called *Gentle Grace*.

When it comes down to it, our convictions are about all we have. They determine who we are. On the other hand, we can't control anyone else, but we don't have to hang with them. It's never too late to say when you're done.

eight

Make Sparks Fly

Here I go, it's all uphill, and I'm taking a ride on a
brand-new road.
Who knows if I'm gonna make it?
But I'm gonna try, try.
All it takes is a new set of wings
To fly, fly.
On my way to a new life
Of new everythings.

—"NEW EVERYTHINGS" BY KATHIE LEE
GIFFORD AND BRETT JAMES

Soon after I moved to NYC in June 1982, I happened to be walking up West End Avenue when I noticed a familiar figure walking down the street toward me. We recognized each other at the exact same moment and said an awkward hello. It was Regis Philbin. Hardly an auspicious meeting. But "little is much when God is in it."

Three years later it was announced that Regis's cohost on *The Morning Show*, Ann Abernathy, was leaving the program to get married. I immediately called Sam to tell him I wanted the job. I was restless and unfulfilled working at *Good Morning America*. Back then everything was on teleprompter and talent was encouraged not to "vary from the script." As an entertainer, I had grown weary of having so little creative freedom.

Somehow it got into the newspapers that I was considering leaving *GMA* to join Regis. I happened to be having lunch one day at Le Cirque restaurant in Midtown when I suddenly noticed the queen of the TV world, Barbara Walters, holding court at a table across the room. I waved obediently and she smiled and beckoned me with her index finger to come over to her table.

I was not close to Barbara or her inner circle, but I admired and respected her, and she had always been pleasant and encouraging to me. "What's this I hear about you joining Regis?" she asked.

"I don't know, Barbara. I want to, but everyone says I'm crazy. Why would I want to leave a major network morning show where I'm poised to get the number-one anchor job to join a local show in New York?"

Barbara didn't miss a beat. "Honey," she said with a chuckle, "Toledo is local."

I paused to consider her words. "If you and Regis click, you won't be local very long."

Of course, she was right.

I auditioned a couple of times and the sparks flew immediately. Soon after, ABC offered me the job.

I couldn't wait to get away from the teleprompter and start playing verbal gymnastics with the master of "television talk." (Working with Regis was akin to playing ping-pong on a tightrope: dangerous and unpredictable but exhilarating.) But I was still technically under contract with *GMA* on the first day of my new cohost gig on *The Morning Show*. I decided to use that technicality for a little comic relief. Just as *GMA* was going off the air at 8:58 a.m. I changed into big sneakers and raced down the street to make a breathless entrance after Regis had already begun at 9:00 a.m. He feigned annoyance at my tardiness and yelled, "Is this the way it's gonna be? Great." And we were off to the races.

There was no one like Regis then and there never will be again. I called him just the other day to touch base with him and Joy during the COVID-19 shutdown. He immediately got on the phone and said, "It's over," in that sardonic Regis style.

I laughed at him and said, "Oh Reege, we had a great run."

"We sure did," he agreed.

We sure did.

nine

Change the World

Some say life is but a whisper, life is but a mist.
Gone before you realize it's true.
But there must be a reason that all things exist.
Some explanation that cannot be dismissed.

—"I HAVE A FIRE" BY KATHIE LEE
GIFFORD FROM *SCANDALOUS*

In the milestones of our lives we discover who we are. If we're blessed with the wisdom that comes with experience, we will also discover our purpose. And then our greater purpose.

Cody was born on March 22, 1990. He was eight pounds, fifteen ounces and delivered by emergency C-section. All babies are blessings, but for me, who had come to believe that I would probably never have a child of my own, he was also a miracle.

Frank already had three grown children when I met him. He was also already a grandfather and certainly didn't want to go through the whole process again. Yet he thought it was completely unfair to deny me the gift of a child if it was something I truly wanted.

I had always loved children, but I was never one of those women who longed to be a mother more than anything else in life. By the time we were married I was thirty-three years old and starting to think my window of opportunity to have healthy babies was closing. I decided to let nature take its course and see where that led.

Honestly, I was so ecstatic to finally be in a loving, supportive, healthy, and sexy relationship that I truly wasn't longing for anything more. Three years after we got married, Frank and I went on a cruise along the Amalfi coast in Italy—one of our favorite places in the world. It was a perfect vacation in every way. One we had looked forward to before the start of the football season and the inevitable time that we would be apart while Frank covered the games.

No one was more surprised than I when, weeks after we returned home, I began to feel a little funny. Not sick, just different. Then something happened that had never happened to me before in my life. I sat before a picnic table full of fresh Maryland blue crabs and couldn't stomach the sight of them. They were and still are one of my favorite foods. I did some math. *When was my last period?* I couldn't remember at first until I realized it had been right before our cruise.

No . . . could it be? How could it be? I was astonished at the possibility after so much time.

We bought a pregnancy test at the drug store and watched the little stick change to a resounding positive. I don't remember being thrilled, and I know for sure that Frank wasn't. But I did eventually rejoice, and so did he, knowing that God was going to bless us with a child.

This was not something we had prayed for, as so many couples do, but something that God had designed for a greater purpose than the fulfillment of our dreams. I had trusted that the Lord would bring it about if it was His will, and it obviously was.

Cody Newton Gifford is now thirty years old, six feet four, and more handsome than ever.

Three months after his birth I took him with me to a small townhouse on the Upper East Side of Manhattan for the dedication of a new facility for newborn babies suffering from HIV or full-blown AIDs. The Variety House for Children was sponsored by the Association to Benefit Children (a-b-c.org). I had been working with Variety, the Children's Charity, for many years and had been particularly impressed by a woman named Gretchen Buchenholz, who had founded the advocacy organization (ABC) years before.

At the time, AIDs was a brand-new, terrifying, and largely misunderstood disease. Just as Diana, princess of Wales, bravely held babies in her arms who were dying from AIDs, so did Gretchen. I was deeply moved by their courage when the rest of the world seemed to be paralyzed by fear of even getting close to these children.

On that hot June day on East Ninety-First Street, I held my very first AIDs baby. He weighed less than two pounds. In my other arm I held my eleven-pound healthy son. One baby born into suffering and pain, the other born into health, prosperity, and hope.

The injustice of that one moment forever changed me. Frank and I both knew that we needed to do more to alleviate the suffering of these children and help Gretchen accomplish her mission.

At that time there was no hope for these babies. They all died. So, day after day, loving, caring volunteers came to the brownstone, now called the Cody House, to simply rock them—literally to love them to death.

That's why Frank and I decided to sue the state of New York to unblind HIV testing so at-risk women could be told their results and given the drugs needed to combat the possibility of their children being born infected with HIV or AIDs. We had learned that if these drugs were administered in utero, the chance of a child being

51

infected went from about 25 percent to less than 8 percent. We had to change the law because although the results of the HIV testing had been tracked, they were not informing the pregnant mothers due to privacy issues.

We were still embroiled in this reality when we received an invitation from my friend Claudia Cohen to attend a dinner at her oceanfront home in East Hampton in 1995. Claudia was aware of our work with the Association to Benefit Children and our ongoing lawsuit with the state of New York, so she purposefully seated me next to New York governor George Pataki.

I took the next two hours to explain to the governor why we were suing the state.

He listened attentively and respectfully and, at the end of our basically one-way conversation, said three things I have never heard a politician say: (1) "I didn't know this," (2) "We're on the wrong side of this issue," and (3) "I'm going to do something about it."

I knew Governor Pataki to be a good, decent man, so I hoped he was sincere. But I also was painfully aware that he would be facing a politically unpopular decision.

At that time gay men were understandably concerned, wanting to keep their HIV status private. There was a terrible stigma surrounding the disease, and they feared for not only their lives but their livelihoods as well. I tried to explain to my many gay friends that this wasn't about them. It was about the babies who had been conceived and had no voice in their own futures. On the other hand, we did have a voice and a responsibility.

Several months later Frank and I stood in the memorial garden of the Cody House and listened as Governor Pataki announced that all HIV testing was to be unblinded. I looked at the paintings of angels and flowers along with the names on the garden walls of children who had been lost to this unspeakable disease. Tears flowed down my cheeks even as I heard protestors chanting outside on the street, "Governor Pataki, we have rights too! Governor Pataki, we have rights too!"

We discovered later that they had been bused in by a political organization hoping to make it onto the evening news. They didn't even understand what they were protesting. They just got paid to do it.

"Forgive them, Father," I remember praying, "for they know not what they do."

One year later the AIDs death rate went down in New York for the first time,[1] which can be attributed to the fact that the AIDs *birth* rate went down. One year later the unblinding of HIV testing was mandated in every state in the nation.

Gretchen and Governor Pataki will forever be two of my all-time personal heroes. They did the right thing for the lives of innocent children, regardless of the social consequences to their own lives.

Soon after our successful lawsuit, Frank and I went to what we came to call "the world's most expensive lunch" with Gretchen. We asked her a simple question: "What more can we do?"

She shared her plan to open a new facility to house the growing number of children, who by then were benefiting from the newly discovered cocktail of drugs that, if administered during their mothers' pregnancies, would help them battle the disease. Frank and I pledged our help. We eventually purchased the Ronald McDonald House on East Eighty-Sixth Street. It had originally been part of an existing church.

For the next year and a half, we attempted to renovate it. But even when you're trying to do a good thing, you come up against all the bureaucracy of any large city that stands in your way. We were denied the permits we needed due to all of the building codes that restricted any possibility of renovation. We had no choice but to tear it down and build from scratch. So we did.

Our daughter, Cassidy, had been born on August 2, 1993, completing our family of four. Gretchen named the new building Cassidy's Place, and on October 24, 1996, we dedicated the four-story, state-of-the-art facility to house all of ABC and care for the growing number of babies living longer with the disease. Today, even as my children prepare to begin their new married lives and start families of their own, the Cody House and Cassidy's Place are alive and well on the East Side of Manhattan.

Changing the world doesn't have to be a large-scale thing—though sometimes small steps inspire major movements. You can impact your neighborhood, the school down the road, or where you work like no one else. It's never too late to change the world, one child at a time.

ten

Sing at the Super Bowl,
Battle Sweatshops, and
Save Your Marriage

Is there some purpose to this time in the darkness?
Lying beneath winter snows?
Will I be stronger, somehow be better?
Only my pillow knows.

—"ONLY MY PILLOW KNOWS" BY KATHIE LEE GIFFORD

The year 1995 started out as one of the best of my life. I had been chosen to sing the national anthem at Super Bowl XXIX in Miami on January 29. ABC would be broadcasting, and Frank would be hosting the telecast live alongside Al Michaels and Dan Dierdorf.

"The Star-Spangled Banner" is one of the most difficult songs to pull off. Don't believe me? Just ask anyone who has performed it. Barry Manilow warned me to not look at the scoreboard because it would show me how many people were tuned in. So factor in the anxiety of, oh, say about a hundred million people watching you attempt it.

Terrifying.

It was time for last looks before heading off to the field to begin the game. With literally seconds to go, my makeup artist unwittingly stuck my left eye with the mascara wand, then my hairdresser, also unwittingly, sprayed hairspray into my right eye. I could not see more than a blur as I was led out before the biggest audience I would ever face.

Frank's voice reverberated all over the stadium.

"Now, to honor America, please join in the singing of our national anthem. . . . Sung by television and recording star, my *wife*, Kathie Lee Gifford."

I couldn't believe he said that. I knew he was proud of me, but it was as if he were confirming to the whole world that the only reason I'd been chosen to sing was because I was sleeping with him. I wanted to kill him! But, of course, I couldn't because I would have had to find him first, and that was impossible since I was now *blind*. Then I heard the boos. They were coming from somewhere in the stadium, but I had no time to process this. The orchestra was playing the introduction.

"Oh, say can you see . . ." I began. "No, I can't!"

Gratefully the song came to a thrilling end as the jets flew overhead, the fireworks exploded, and the audience went crazy. There were no more boos, and somehow I was shuffled off the field and onto a plane to go home. I soon discovered that Howard Stern had asked his fans to boo me when I was introduced.

The whole experience was completely surreal, as so many moments in my life have been.

Then in March 1996 my world came crashing in. A man stood up in Congress and accused me of operating sweatshops in

Honduran factories to manufacture my Walmart clothing line. He represented himself as a human rights activist, when in reality, he worked for UNITE, a garment industry lobby that desperately wanted to unionize the world's largest retailer.

I was obviously blindsided. In six months we would be opening Cassidy's Place after spending several years of our lives building it and millions of our dollars paying for it—most of the money coming from, yes, my Walmart profits.

All hell broke loose. Nobody cared about the truth. Nobody. I went to every network I had worked for—including my employer at the time, ABC. To their shame, and my disbelief, not one of them reported the truth about my accuser's lies or the truth about him. The vicious attacks went on for months with no sign of letting up. We turned off the TV and avoided grocery and convenience stores— everywhere and anywhere that the dreaded tabloids peddled their poison. I can't imagine going through this kind of hell in the social media world we live in today.

There were calls for me to be fired from *Live with Regis and Kathie Lee*. Thankfully ABC understood that the accusations were false and designed to ultimately damage Walmart's reputation with no regard to mine.

I was grateful for their support but still hurt when they refused to cover my accuser's apology to me and my family. During the darkest period of the insanity my longtime friend Larry King called to ask me to come on his show. I knew he would be fair because both Frank and I had always been treated fairly by him in the past.

Larry asked me whether my sales had taken a hit in light of all these baseless accusations, and I told him that, actually, it was quite the opposite. They had gone through the roof.

"Really?" he asked. He was genuinely shocked to hear this.

"Yes," I confirmed and proceeded to tell him how just the other day at my show a lady had stood up and gestured to the outfit she was wearing. I recognized it immediately as a dress from my Walmart collection.

"You look great," I told her.

She said, "When that man stood up in Congress and accused you like that, I got so mad I went straight to Walmart and bought five of your dresses!"

I am so grateful to all the people who continued to believe in me and continued to trust my heart through the most difficult times of my life.

I penned these lyrics at the darkest moment in this experience:

Have you ever felt tossed and alone on a sea of despair?
Have you ever felt lost but you know that you're going nowhere?
Ever felt that the truth was nowhere to be found?
Ever felt like screaming but you can't make a sound?[2]

All of my lyrics come from the truth I have discovered.

Finally, after diving in to fight *real* sweatshops, we got laws passed to protect against the abuses. The "hot goods" provision of the Fair Labor Standards Act, which had languished in Albany, New York, for nine years, was passed in nine days when Frank and I got involved. I spent a year commuting to Washington, DC, to sit with President Clinton to form an alliance between retailers and (real) human rights advocates. I testified before Congress, an audience I never dreamed I'd have (and didn't enjoy at all, trust me).

As bad as 1996 was, 1997 was far worse and the pain much closer to home. I was already deeply wounded and battle scarred from the public execution that had resulted after the previous year's unfounded accusations. Some people still believed, in spite of all the evidence to the contrary, that I knowingly and willfully ran sweatshops. I finally had to accept that these people would never change their opinions because the false narrative somehow fit their agenda.

Frank and I emerged from the assault even stronger as a couple. He had been my champion and closest friend throughout the ordeal. He was my hero—until one day when everything changed.

On May 1, 1997, Frank met a woman at the Regency Hotel on Park Avenue in New York City and committed adultery. He had been set up to be caught by a revolting tabloid magazine.

I can't say it any more plainly, and even writing those words all this time later pains me.

For years I avoided driving down Park Avenue, hoping to avoid the natural emotions it would trigger.

Soon after I learned the truth, I wrote the lyrics to "Only My Pillow Knows":

> There is no distance so close as two lovers
> Face to face skin against skin.
> There is no pleasure so deep as together.
> They breathe letting no one else in.
>
> Now there's no distance so great
> As two people in the same bed, worlds apart.
> There is no chasm so steep as betrayal,
> No damage so deep to a heart. . . .
>
> CHORUS:
> Go ask the river that's run here so long.
> Go ask the sparrow that still sings its song.
> Go ask the willow that bends though wind blows.
> But only my pillow knows.

I also began sessions with a trusted counselor. Frank immediately asked me to forgive him and I did. I had to. My whole faith is built on the foundation of forgiveness: Jesus died for *me* for the forgiveness of *my* sins. We cannot withhold from others what He has freely given to us.

But I struggled with the casual way in which Frank expected us to get on with our lives—as if nothing had happened. I couldn't automatically feel the same way about him that I always had. He wasn't my hero anymore. When I shared this with my therapist one day, he said words that are now emblazoned on my heart:

"Kathie, if you can't forgive your husband, forgive your children's father."

It was a revelatory moment. It took my eyes off of me and set them squarely on my children, who were still completely unaware of their father's unfaithfulness. My children's father was a wonderful, loving, gentle, compassionate, generous, and sweet man. He was easy to forgive because I knew his heart.

Now, with new eyes to see, I prayed an almost impossible prayer. "Lord, please give me a deeper desire for Frank than I have ever had for him, even more than at the beginning."

This was an epic request. I was *crazy* in love with Frank then, and grateful to finally have the kind of exciting, thrilling, ecstatic love I'd only known about from books or movies.

To my surprise, God answered my prayer and gave me a desire for Frank unlike anything we had ever experienced. Every time we made love it was truly healing for me.

"Now I see how you're gonna get back at me, Kathie. You're gonna kill me," he loved to say.

The laughter returned, and our children grew up to be the most extraordinary two human beings I've ever known. By the time they learned the truth of what had happened, they knew an even deeper truth: their parents loved them and each other enough to trust in God's healing.

Our lives can take some unexpected twists and turns. Some come as the result of our choices; other times it's because of someone else's. No matter how hard things might become, it's never too late to bring beauty from the ashes. If you find yourself in such a place as I did—in the midst of a season of great difficulty—take a deep breath, prayerfully face the truth, find a Christian counselor to help you figure out your next steps, and trust God to lead you through.

eleven
Let Go

Your Word, Your Word
It heals like a balm,
Rebukes the howling winds and
Makes the waters calm.
It's the power, the power
Of Your Word.

—"YOUR WORD" BY KATHIE LEE GIFFORD

Frank and I were not the only ones to think 1997 was a difficult year. His daughter Vicki was in the throes of a painful divorce from her husband, Michael Kennedy. It was especially brutal because of the nonstop tabloid attention. We all did everything we could to shield Vicki and her three children from the onslaught of the vicious media frenzy, but that's most often a losing battle.

We invited Vicki and the kids to join us at our home in Colorado over the holidays. We lived at the top of an over eight-thousand-foot mountain in a development with a big gate and a round-the-clock security guard. Sadly, that couldn't keep out the heartache that was about to happen.

While Vicki and the kids were staying with us, Michael was with the whole Kennedy clan that regularly descended on Aspen for the holidays. Michael called Vicki to ask that the children be allowed to join him for the New Year's festivities. She reluctantly agreed because, while at that point there was virtually no hope for their devastated marriage, she truly desired to save her children's relationship with their father.

Late in the afternoon on New Year's Eve we received a phone call telling us that Michael had been skiing backward down a steep slope tossing a football back and forth to other skiers. He had hit a tree and was now hanging on to life in the emergency room at the Aspen hospital.

Vicki was at a movie theater in Vail seeing *Titanic*, so Frank jumped in the car and drove like crazy to find her. He spotted her in the audience, pulled her out to tell her the terrible news, and drove her back west toward our house, where I met them at the bottom of the mountain. I had grabbed my makeup case for the trip to Aspen, some two hours away, because there was no way I was going to let the paparazzi get any lucrative pictures of the "hysterical grieving widow" they're so famous for.

Vicki, understandably, was in shock. Frank drove and I sat in the back seat with her, where she finally vomited. Then I got to work. As we were trying to navigate the icy mountain highway, I talked softly to her and prayed intermittently while attempting to apply her makeup. We were about halfway to Aspen when we got the news that Michael had been declared brain dead.

Vicki heaved heartbroken tears. She had loved Michael since she was fifteen years old, and although he had betrayed her and left her emotionally destroyed, she had never wished him harm. She would always love him.

I did her makeup once again and finished just as we were pulling up to the emergency room entrance.

It was completely still. Not a person, not a car, not an ambulance in sight. Eerily silent.

Apparently, the news hadn't broken, and Aspen was still in full-on New Year's Eve revelry.

Vicki and Frank entered the hospital. I stayed in the car with a phone in case the children called. Eventually I had to use the bathroom, so I quietly walked in to find one—that coincidentally ended up being directly across from the room where Frank and Vicki were with Michael's body.

As I came out of the ladies' room I found myself standing directly across from Ethel Kennedy, still in her ski suit but disheveled, with her jacket hanging from her waist. The look on her face was one of utter and total shock. I wish I could erase it from my memory, but I can't.

It was the same look we'd all seen so many times before, after her husband, Robert F. Kennedy, was murdered by Sirhan Sirhan in 1968 right in front of her at the Ambassador Hotel in Los Angeles. *My God*, I thought, *how much can one woman take?* I quietly walked over to her and embraced her and whispered how sorry I was. She had always been very candid that Michael was her favorite child of the eleven she had borne. And now he, too, was gone.

I returned to wait in the car but soon received a call asking me to please tell Vicki the children needed her. I had no choice but to go back into the hospital to tell her. I whispered into her ear that someone had sent a car for her, and she left immediately to attend to her children.

That left Frank and me alone with Ethel and Michael's body on a table. I didn't want to look at him, but it was impossible not to— and not to notice the back of his head. It was a color I had never seen before and I pray to God I never see again. It was the color of death.

For more than an hour Ethel did not move from his side. She

did not say a word, she did not cry a tear, but she did refuse to leave her son's lifeless body, shaking her head adamantly when anyone came in to try to convince her to depart.

I looked at Frank as if to ask, "What are we going to do?"

He looked at me helplessly. He had known Ethel for years and knew that no one could get Ethel Kennedy to do anything she wasn't ready to do.

I prayed silently, *Dear God, please comfort this poor woman. Dear God—*

And then I leaned over to her and gently whispered, "It's okay, Ethel. You can leave him. Michael's not there, he's not there. He's with God."

She didn't move or respond, as if she hadn't heard a word I'd said. That's when I added, "To be absent from the body is to be present with the Lord."

Suddenly, she turned her head toward me. "What did you say?"

Again I said, "To be absent from the body is to be present with the Lord."

She was stunned. "Where did you hear that?"

"It's from the Bible, Ethel, in Second Corinthians five" (v. 8, author paraphrase).

"I never heard that," she said simply and began to struggle with her ski suit.

Frank signaled to me that I should leave so he could be there with her when she finally said goodbye to her cherished son for the last time.

I gently squeezed her arm and left the room, marveling yet again at God and how He works through His Word. All I had done was quote from the Scriptures—God's Word. The Bible says that His Word never returns void (Isa. 55:11). It is alive and active, and it penetrates deep down into our souls, way beyond the joints and marrow of our bodies. Ethel had gone to Mass every day of her life, including that morning before she went to ski with her family. But she had never heard those words before—the only words that could comfort her heart long enough to give her the strength to move away from her beloved son.

Days later Michael was buried in Boston, Massachusetts. Every member of the Kennedy family was there, of course, including John F. Kennedy Jr. and his wife, Carolyn Bessette. She nodded silently toward me and I smiled a sad smile back at her.

Two years later, on July 16, 1999, they, too, would be gone after their plane crashed into the Atlantic Ocean off Martha's Vineyard. Yet another Kennedy tragedy. Vicki never married again, but all three of her children did, and she now has five beautiful grandchildren she cherishes.

God is faithful. God redeems.

It's never too late to let go because we can trust God to make all things new.

twelve

Leave a Good Thing

The sky's growing darker as the evening draws near.
The storm clouds have gathered
And the shadows are gone.
When all hope has faded,
Replaced now with fear,
Tell me what can we depend on?
We can depend on His Word
When all hope is gone
We can still depend on,
We can depend on His Word.

—"WE CAN DEPEND ON HIS WORD"
BY KATHIE LEE GIFFORD

Many years ago, so many I can't remember, I was singing a song into my father's movie camera. (This was ages before the iPhone.) I stopped singing a capella at one point and said, "Where's da moo-sic, Daddy?" I can still hear my daddy so tenderly respond, "Oh, honey, you have to learn to make your own music."

It has taken me a lifetime to learn to make my own music.

For decades I sang and recorded hundreds of songs by brilliant composers—everyone from Joni Mitchell to the Bergmans, Sondheim, Hamlisch, and others, never dreaming that my father literally meant what he'd said. Sure, I'd written silly songs my whole life, little ditties and novelty songs. But, as is often the case, one day it all crystalized.

I had just closed on Broadway. I had been taking over for Carol Burnett for three months in a Sondheim "review" called *Putting It Together*—one of the most profound professional experiences of my lifetime. It was exhausting but thrilling.

Right before my debut, a stagehand strike was looming, and it looked like I might not get the chance to actually perform. I did my one and only run-through with the cast, costume, sound, and the orchestra, then went to my dressing room to await the legendary Stephen Sondheim and be the recipient of his even more legendary "notes" on my performance. As I waited alone for that knock on my door, I had a few moments to ponder the extraordinary significance of the moment I was living in: about to make my lifetime dream of performing on a Broadway stage come true. It was mind-blowing to me.

Stephen arrived and graciously praised my performance, giving me (blessedly) just a few benign notes.

"That's it?" I asked him, incredulously.

"That's it," he responded. "Just show up."

And then I said to him, "You know, Stephen, even if I never get to make my Broadway debut, I will have gotten from this experience everything I could have ever dreamed."

He nodded. "Because you did the work."

The strike was averted, and I did debut on December 7, 1999, to the best reviews of my life. Something I wasn't used to at all, believe me. Executive producer Rob Burnett had been in the audience my closing night. The next day he called me and asked me to be the first woman to host *Late Night with David Letterman.*

I was stunned but flattered. I said something like, "You bet your ass, mister."

After hosting the Letterman show, I knew without a doubt I was to move on from *Live with Regis and Kathie Lee* and into a whole new season of my creative life. I remember clearly hearing the Lord's voice above the audience's applause after my monologue. "Take a mental picture, Kathie," He said to me. "This is the moment your life changed."

The next day I told Regis. Hard as it was for both of us, he understood. Then I announced my decision on the air on Monday.

People think you're either crazy or incredibly ungrateful when you walk away from that kind of success. I was neither. I was totally grateful for the unprecedented opportunity I had had with Regis and equally grateful for the thrilling yet unknown opportunities that awaited me.

I *had* to leave. Artists die on the vine unless they are creating, and I had already squeezed every ounce of creative juice I had out of my fifteen amazing years with my dear friend and partner.

I had been in a velvet rut: making TV history, making a boatload of money, yet dying inside to get to those big-bucket dreams. It was time. So I walked away in July 2000 to an unknown but exciting future.

But nothing ever actually turns out the way you think it will, does it?

Sometimes it's even better.

Think about your own hopes and dreams. Is there something you've put up on a shelf, telling yourself, "Maybe someday" or "I could never do that . . ."? It might be time to dust that thing off and take another look. Or maybe, like me, you find yourself in a velvet rut that simply makes it too easy to stay. Give yourself the gift of dreaming because it's never too late to leave a good thing.

thirteen

Seek the Truth

They put you on a game show and you la la out a
    tune.
It's swell. You sell!
They put you in commercials and you promise folks
    the moon.
It's swell. You sell!

—"YOU SELL" BY KATHIE LEE GIFFORD

I hate the phrase *reinvent yourself.* And I'm not fond of the word *retire.* I prefer re-*fire.* For how can I reinvent myself when I never invented myself to begin with? God created me, and He created you too. Acts 17 says, "in him we live and move and have our being" (v. 28).

So when I left *Live with Regis and Kathie Lee*, I didn't retire. I moved on to the next stage of my life. I concentrated on other interests. I recorded two CDs, *Heart of a Woman* for Universal Records and *Born for You* on my own label, On the Lamb Records. The first one flopped and the second one didn't. That's the yin and yang and ebb and flow of the business.

I continued my work in theater and opened the musical *Under the Bridge* at the Zipper Theatre in 2005. I have a distinct memory of watching Rosie O'Donnell and Donald and Melania Trump seated next to each other in the front row. Rosie and Donald were sharing M&M's, chatting, and getting along just fine. Ah, the good old days!

I first met Donald Trump when I arrived in New York City in June 1982 to begin work on *Good Morning America*. He was already a fixture in New York society and a powerhouse mover and shaker in business. He was bigger than life and often the center of both personal and professional scandal. Some people adored him; some people loathed him. Some things never change.

But here's the thing I learned: never believe what you hear or read about someone. The media is generated by an insatiable lust for power, prestige, and most importantly, money.

The first real professional song I ever wrote, called "You Sell," was a commentary on this theme. I performed it at Rainbow and Stars at the top of Rockefeller Center for two weeks in my cabaret act and also in my monologue when I hosted *Late Night with David Letterman*.

They put you on a game show and you la la out a tune.
It's swell. You sell!
They put you in commercials and you promise folks the moon.
It's swell. You sell!
They put you next to Regis and you talk about your life.
You fight so much together people think that you're his wife.
It's swell. You sell!

They put you on the cover and say you're cryin' the blues.
It sells! It sells!
They say you're leaving Regis, that's supposed to be news?
It sells! It sells!

They put you on the cover and say your marriage is over!
They put you on the cover and say your husband's a rover!
They put you on the cover, say your kid is a brat!
You once were anorexic, but now you're getting fat!
They put you on the cover and say, "She's cryin' again,"
And the source, of course, is always a "close personal friend."
The next day you're battling with Rosie and pills.
The next day you're going broke because of all the bills.
But that's because of all the plastic surgery you've had.
And now you're close to suicide because it turned out bad.

How do I stay alive with all those cancer scares?
How do I keep on smiling when greeted by those stares?
How do I manage sanity while facing all those lies?
How do I manage motherhood and keep those awesome thighs?
Who cares? Who cares?

There must be something missing from somebody's life
When they'd rather read about the plight of Frank Gifford's wife.
Is this really what's become of what used to be news?
Perhaps the thing they're missing is a Carnival cruise.
Hey, they put that fire out very fast!

But why is everybody always picking on me?
Please tell! Please tell!
Why am I the butt of all those jokes on TV?
It's hell! It's hell!

I really shouldn't take it so personally.
To them I'm not a person but a personality.

BAND:
You sell!

Yeah, swell.
The critics and the pundits ponder endlessly
When, oh God, please when will we be rid of Kathie Lee?
I wish they had the answer, if they only had a clue.
I nearly died of shock from Broadway when I got a good review.
(Actually, it wasn't good, it was an absolute rave!)
But it'll never happen again, my future is secure.
I'll keep on filling pages that smell faintly of manure.

BAND:
It smells!

Shh! It sells!
They'll all be filled with jealousy and misery and vice
'Cause they can deal with any news except the kind that's nice!
You know in all sincerity
I treat it with hilarity.
It helps me keep my sanity,
Maintain my famous vanity.
I've learned to laugh at critics and to scoff at all the jests.
Yes, the press is tough, the paparazzi are just pests.
But you people have been great to me.
You're the reason that I stay.
With a lot of help from heaven
And a lot of chardonnay.

BAND:
She drinks!

Not all day!
They take your picture when you're simply scratchin' your eye,
Then print "there she goes again startin' to cry,"
When in fact you're really laughing 'cause you know it isn't true.
They're writing about someone, but that someone isn't you.

If I believed the crap I read,
How I'm a woman filled with greed
Who really is a heartless jerk,
Who loves to put small kids to work,
The hissy fits,
The phony bits,
The phony bitch with phony tits,
Who slept her way up to the top,
And talks and talks and just won't stop
I'd hate me too!

I loved watching the audiences' reaction to the words as they recognized the truth in them. The tabloids wrote all kinds of garbage about me because, for some inexplicable reason, I sold millions of dollars of magazines and newspapers for them.

The tabloids only exist because there's a huge, voracious appetite in our culture to consume garbage. We put trash in our bodies every day in the form of junk food. We also put trash into our minds when we purchase salacious and unsubstantiated gossip. It doesn't really matter if any of it is true or not; all that matters is that it sells. And it will sell until the next person arrives on the scene and it starts all over again under a new name.

If I hadn't been able to hold on to my own truth through all the viciousness of those years, I'd be in the Betty Ford Center, or in prison, or dead. But I didn't let the headlines define me. I battled every day to keep reminding myself that only God could do that. And every day I clung for dear life to what His Word said about me.

I have known many of the people who have been swept up in the headlines over the last four decades. Many I consider friends; others are colleagues. It has pained me to watch how the lies have damaged some of their reputations and livelihoods. In cases when I knew the accusations to be true, I was pleased to see them brought to justice.

Many innocent people have been destroyed, and too many truly guilty people are still walking around freely, continuing to use their power to abuse others. It's infuriating, isn't it? I understand why so many scream at their radios and TVs, lashing out at all the insanity.

There is something very basic and primal in us that longs for justice. But that, too, has been perverted in our culture. Because if we don't care about justice *for all*, we don't really care about it *at all*, do we?

My point is this: I continue to believe in the truth about the people I have known personally and privately. And that truth has rarely been what I heard or read anywhere else. It's never too late to pause to consider whether some salacious piece of "news" might not actually be true at all.

fourteen

Make a Toast

Guy: I'll bring the whiskey.
Girl: I'll bring the wine.
Guy: I'll get my guitar.
Girl: I'll go and get mine. I'll wear my new lace.
Guy: I'll wear my old leather.
Together: Yeah, we were made to make music
    together.

—"WHISKEY AND WINE" BY KATHIE LEE

GIFFORD FROM *THEN CAME YOU*

I was born in Paris, France, but my parents weren't the least bit French, so neither am I. As I mentioned earlier, we were in France because my daddy was in the navy. He had been assigned a position with General Dwight D. Eisenhower's staff at SHAPE (Supreme Headquarters Allied Powers Europe).

My parents had never been to Europe, so they embraced everything they experienced while they were there—all of the European traditions as well as traveling every chance they had to explore the wonders of England, Germany, Italy, and Switzerland. When they finally did return to America, they brought their memories and their newfound affection for the delicacies they had discovered. Most especially, wine.

I grew up in this environment. I have wonderful memories of watching them enjoy a bottle of chianti with my mother's spaghetti or a classic chardonnay with her roasted chicken. I associate wine with beautiful family memories, which has had a profound effect on my own sensibilities about the abundant life.

Wine is the most commonly mentioned alcoholic beverage in the Bible. It is a source of symbolism, yes, but it was also a deeply important part of Judaic life during biblical times. Interestingly, the ancient Hebrews also drank beer;[3] just like my daddy discovered when he was transferred from Paris to Wiesbaden, Germany.

We had a loving home with parents who celebrated God's blessings every day. It was joyful, it was celebratory, and it was fun. That is, unless my father was in the doghouse for something or my brother, Dave, was being a pain. Then you could expect that delicious roasted chicken to be thrown right at them by my mother. Yep, Joanie was a drama queen and full of surprises. But she usually missed, thank God.

One day in 2015, a very big man named Andy Cohan (no, not that one—slightly different spelling) came to meet with me at the NBC studios. My attorney had set up the meeting, and I was looking forward to hearing what this man had to say.

His first question was, "Why aren't you in the wine business?"

"Where have you been all my life?" was my obvious response.

Andy was there to suggest a partnership with a successful company called Scheid Family Wines, located in Monterey County, California. At that time, they produced grapes for eighty different boutique wines. Francis Ford Coppola was among their clients, so they were a highly reputable company. Andy suggested a fifty-fifty partnership wherein Scheid would grow, manufacture, and bottle my wines, and I would participate in the selection, packaging, and promotion of them.

"Kathie," he warned me right off the bat, "this isn't going to be easy. There's a very healthy cynicism out there regarding celebrity wines. People think celebrities just slap their names on their labels and cash a fat check. That's what you'll be up against, so this is going to take time."

"I get it," I told him. "But I want to be a serious partner. Someone might buy a bottle of my wine the first time out of curiosity, but they're never going to buy another one if it isn't excellent."

"Exactly," he agreed. And we made the deal.

I named my wines GIFFT not only because it contains letters from my own name but also as a play on the word *gift*—which I believe all blessings are.

I had an unusual way of choosing the wines we wanted to green-light for Scheid to produce. Everyone in my household had to taste the samples Scheid sent, and we had to agree unanimously on the winner. We all loved the process and never disagreed on the final choice for our red blend, chardonnay, rosé, and pinot grigio, which have all gone on to win double gold medals in blind taste tests in California wine competitions.

Our latest varietal is a delicious peach-flavored sparkling rosé—just in time to be served at my children's weddings. But the best news of all is that our 4,800-acre Scheid Vineyards in beautiful Greenfield, California, just won one of the most prestigious wine-industry awards in the state—the California Green Medal environment award for being the cleanest, most sustainable, most energy-efficient vineyard.

I had to call GIFFT wine my "stuff" on the air with Hoda due to FCC rules. People always asked us if we were actually drinking wine on the show. No, I always answered honestly, we were *sipping* GIFFT wine, just as my father taught me. But so you'll know, being involved with a morning show means waking up at two o'clock in the morning. So it's not like we'd fall out of bed and begin belting back the vino. Actually, it was not our idea to have wine on the host chat table. For that you can thank, or curse, Chelsea Handler.

Chelsea was an early guest on our fourth hour soon after I joined the show. She was there to promote a new book, *Are You There, Vodka? It's Me, Chelsea.* The producers had prepared a veritable plethora of vodka cocktails as a prop for her segment, and, let's give them credit, it worked beautifully.

A week later, Brooke Shields showed up and immediately asked, "Where's my cocktail?"

The next week Joel McHale showed up carrying his own bottle of Hennessy, which he promptly began to imbibe without the use of a glass. It got the producers' attention, and suddenly one day two glasses of GIFFT wine magically appeared on our table.

Hoda and I laughed and had some fun with it, thinking it was all a big joke and would soon pass. It didn't. The audience loved it and our ratings began to climb. *USA Today* christened us "The Happy Hour of Daytime TV," and we were off and running. Hoda and I were stunned that nobody at NBC put a stop to it, but no one said a word.

It took on a life of its own.

I've been gone from the show for more than a year, but the two glasses of wine still remain in front of Hoda and Jenna. I think it's the best example of the fact that it's never too late to toast!

fifteen
Celebrate

Little by little God chiseled at my heart
Tearing down the walls that had kept us apart.
And little by little I finally came to see
The man He sees when He looks at me.
That man I always wanted to be.

—"ENLIGHTENED" BY KATHIE LEE GIFFORD

Frank had a strong, deeply rooted religious upbringing. His parents were Pentecostal Christians, and every time they moved to a new place, they found the closest Assembly of God church and put their three children in Sunday school.

Weldon Gifford, Frank's father, was an oil worker and often out of work. It was the 1930s and the Great Depression had ravaged many a family all over the country. The Giffords moved twenty-nine times. We know this from Frank's mother's Bible, which chronicled every move. It was a bleak and difficult time for them—even having to, at times, eat dog food to survive. But they were grateful for it.

Every time the family moved Frank would establish himself in the new community with his athletic prowess. He was deeply competitive with his older brother, Waine, and usually dominated in any game the neighbors were playing. His older sister, Winona, was a strong-willed but brilliant young woman.

The family finally settled in Bakersfield, California, when Frank was in high school. He was the youngest of the three children and the first Gifford to graduate from high school, much less graduate from college—which he did as an All-American Trojan football player at the University of Southern California.

Always an athlete, Frank played football every chance he got. His high school grades weren't strong enough to gain the athletic scholarship he needed for college, so he attended Bakersfield Junior College, played a season of football there, and got his grades up to what was required for him to enroll at USC.

I remember him telling me about it early in our friendship. "See, Kathie, real men went into the oil fields. They didn't play sissy games like football."

A man among men, Frank grew up believing in a big, all-powerful God of the universe, but he never understood what it meant to have a personal relationship with the living God. Not until we went to Israel in 2012 with our dear friends Emilie and Craig Wierda. That experience changed everything for Frank. He got baptized in the Jordan River he'd heard so much about back in Sunday school decades before.

Life with Frank was a lot of things, but one thing it wasn't was boring. Early in our marriage I started to be introduced to the myriad of misfits, miscreants, and all-out crazy creatures who made up his world. I was, for the most part, fascinated by them.

One of the most colorful by far was Evel Knievel, the infamous daredevil who defied gravity and sanity but kept the world breathless with his exploits. He called often for Frank and would talk on for hours. Frank loved him; he had covered almost all of Evel's jumps in ABC's *Wide World of Sports*, and they had become good friends over the years.

Evel's career had made him a media and cultural darling, but his private exploits were sometimes more than Frank could endure, especially for hours at a time. After a while on the phone with him, Frank would suddenly say, "You know, Evel, talk to Kathie. She loves this stuff."

I'd look at him like, "What?" but take the phone and Evel would just continue with his tale. I really liked Evel—I appreciated his uniqueness and his honesty.

Most of the time the subject of our conversations would turn to religion. I tried unsuccessfully for years to convince Evel that I hated the baggage that comes with organized religion, and I attempted to steer him to other more positive aspects, but he was better at talking than listening. Our one-sided conversations would go something like this:

"Kathie, I hate Jesus."

"I know you do, Evel, but *why* do you hate Jesus? What did Jesus ever do to you?"

And he would launch into a diatribe about his kids, his ex-wives, doctors, or the media—whatever it happened to be that had infuriated him that particular day.

It always ended the same way, with me saying, "Evel, I'm praying for you. Lots of people who love you are praying for you, and one day you're going to call me out of the blue and say, 'Kathie, you're right! I don't hate Jesus, I *love* Him.'"And then he'd laugh and hang up the phone.

I answered the phone one day in 2012 to hear Evel's familiar voice literally screaming, "Kathie! You were right! I accepted Jesus. He's real, and He loves me. Let me talk to Frank!"

It was surreal. Evel got on the phone with Frank and talked his ear off about his real-life leap—but this was one of faith. Frank was tickled by it.

"Kath," he said afterward, "did I ever tell you about Evel's worst jump?"

"No. What happened?"

"It was in London in 1975 at Wembley Stadium. He was supposed to jump over thirteen buses. The night before the telecast we walked into the stadium to survey the site. There were the thirteen buses lined up. Evel looked at the ramp for a long time. Then he looked at me and said, 'Frank, I can't do it. I can make it over twelve but not thirteen.'

"I asked him, 'Are you sure, Evel?'

"'Yep,' he said, as if it were the most natural thing in the world.

"'Well, Evel, if you're sure you can't make it, you have to cancel the jump.'

"'No, I can't cancel,' he said. 'But I can't make the jump.'"

"Frank!" I shouted in the middle of the story. "Why not?"

"''Cause he said he'd do it. That was Evel."

"What happened?" I asked, almost afraid to know.

"He didn't make it. Exactly as he said would happen. He hit the thirteenth bus and went flying in the air for yards. People thought he was dead. But as they carried him out of the stadium, he lifted up his arm and the crowd went wild. I rushed over to him, and as I leaned in he grabbed me and pulled me close. Obviously concerned about more than how his latest stunt had ended, Evel said, 'Frank, get that broad out of my hotel room.'"

It was one of Frank's all-time favorite stories to tell. Not only was it classic Evel Knievel, it was proof that anyone can make a leap of faith.

Frank, who had also come to know Jesus late in his extraordinary life, came home from Israel a changed man. He'd often say to me, "You know what, honey, I'm not afraid to die. I'm actually starting to get very curious." And though no one ever wants to talk about their own death, he told me many times that he did not want to be buried. He was claustrophobic. "Don't put me in a box," he'd insist. "And promise you'll pull the plug if anyone starts to wipe my buns."

I'd always chuckle and say, "Frank, I love you very much, but I'm not going to go to prison for you."

"Then just trip over it and make it look like an accident."

He also was very clear that he did not want a funeral. He hated funerals. He buried way too many people he loved in his almost eighty-five years.

"Just throw me a big party in the backyard, serve GIFFT wine, and blare Sinatra. And only invite people I actually care about. No assholes. Oh, and don't let anyone tell sad stories and start crying. Only funny ones."

He died on a Sunday morning in 2015 one week shy of his eighty-fifth birthday. Three days later we threw him a party—exactly the kind he wanted.

The following Monday I returned to *TODAY* and shared the hope of eternal life that Frank had discovered through Jesus' sacrifice on the cross. Millions of people saw it. What I didn't share at that time was that we had decided as a family to offer Frank's brain to be studied before he was cremated.

Boston University was conducting exhaustive research on CTE—chronic traumatic encephalopathy. This hideous disease is caused by repeated concussions, which result in damage to the brain. Frank's brain tissue was invaluable to the study.

Several months later we were told that, yes, as we expected, Frank's brain was riddled with CTE, but the portion that wasn't affected, known as heavy matter, was as healthy as a twenty-year-old's.

Through the years he had stayed fit, active, and interested in life. He read constantly and learned new things every day. He loved deeply and was deeply loved in return.

Frank Gifford was not just a football player turned sportscaster; he was a child of God. And his death was when his greatest adventure, and celebration, began.

sixteen

Have Beautiful Feet

What is this wondrous gift I've been given?
It's too marvelous to even comprehend.
Who am I that this Savior would love me forever?
Give me joy beyond measure, and peace without end?
What grace, amazing grace.

—"WHAT GRACE" BY KATHIE LEE GIFFORD AND CHUCK
HARMONY & CLAUDE KELLY OF LOUIS YORK

I love stories. Everyone has them, and it's a gift to listen to others tell theirs. People come alive when they share their stories. And they feel validated that someone wants to hear them.

You want to feel *really* good? Go into a nursing home or a hospital and ask the people you meet to tell you their story. For some of them—and probably way too many—it will be the first time anyone has asked. And, oh, what stories most *all* of them have to tell.

When I first joined *TODAY* it was with the understanding that I would be allowed to bring my love for theater—which is actually storytelling—to a live television audience. I'm grateful to our executive producer at the time, Jim Bell, for honoring that commitment.

My desire was to have a monthly segment called "Everyone Has a Story" in which our viewers would submit their personal accounts and we would choose one to turn into a song. Then we would welcome the viewer to our sofa and perform the song that my writing partner, David Friedman, and I had created. Sung by the greatest singers in the world: Broadway stars!

In eleven years we wrote one hundred "Everyone Has a Story" songs and saw one hundred ordinary people with extraordinary lives respond in real time. It was a total joy and privilege to bring these unique experiences to life.

When I was growing up, I was fascinated by my parents' life stories. They were heartbreaking but ultimately triumphant, as all the best ones are.

Both of my parents' childhoods were like Dickens novels—child abandoned, child abused, child unloved, and child left hopeless until . . . love showed up and changed everything.

My father's Russian/Jewish immigrant father abandoned his wife and five young children. He drank too much and ran around too much—an all-too-common tale then and now.

My mother's mother died of tuberculosis when my mom was two, followed a year later by my mother's only brother, who died from measles. The stock market had crashed, and my mother's father had lost his fortune and successful career in publishing. He, too, took to alcohol to numb the pain and soon married an equally wounded woman who shared his addictions. Once a classical violinist, my maternal grandfather descended into a haze of despair ending in frequent booze-fueled fights with his wife and trips to jail in the "paddy wagon." My mom, Joanie, and her sister, Marilyn, had to go in the paddy wagon as well because there was no one to care for them.

My grandfather died when my mother was nine years old. Joanie's sense of shame was born of such events. Her whole life she would battle a profound but deeply embedded lie in her soul: she wasn't loved, she wasn't good enough, and she was unworthy of happiness. Her grandmother was the only light in her broken life.

Quite old already and crippled with rheumatoid arthritis in her feet, my great-grandmother struggled to care for her two young granddaughters and teach them how to survive in such a heartless, brutally unfair world. Then she, too, died when Joanie was fifteen. Mom's sister, Marilyn, had married young and moved away. Joanie was truly alone in the world.

Because of this, Joanie had to drop out of school and go to work at the local five-and-dime store, living in her one and only girl-friend's house and forced to give almost every cent she earned to the friend's mother to help pay the rent. Into this hopelessness, love arrived in the form of a lanky, athletic, hardworking young naval petty officer, my daddy, Eppie Epstein.

My dad literally rescued my mom from that house and took her home to his. His family rejected her, too, but Daddy loved and protected her for the next fifty-four years.

My daddy's father, Meyer "Sam" Epstein, was a complicated man. Although he was by all accounts a terrible husband and father, he had a reputation as a warm and generous man to the neediest in his neighborhood. I can't imagine what my daddy had to do to reconcile his father's coldness and emotional abuse with the out-pouring of affection his father displayed to total strangers.

Sam Epstein was a Jew by birth and heritage, but he was not a reli-gious man. My father's mother, Evelyn, was not religious either. But one very hot and sticky summer day, when my father was eight, she sent all five of her children to the church down the street when she had reached her limit and couldn't take any more of their rowdiness.

That's how my father found himself at Vacation Bible School asking Jesus into his heart. Seven years later, when he was walking around the Maryland State House in Annapolis, a gang of young hooligans attacked him, throwing rocks at him and screaming, "Christ killer! Christ killer! Christ killer!" It breaks my heart now to think of the terrible confusion my father had to live with because of his last name and heritage.

When my dad was fourteen years old, he went to work and gave all the money he made to his mother so she could buy an old used car. Evelyn eventually married again, only to lose her husband, David, and her oldest son, Paul, in World War II. Her middle son, Carol (pronounced Carl), was wounded. Only my daddy returned home from the war unscathed physically, but he was deeply affected emotionally.

Unlike Mom, Daddy never spoke of the past. He suffered privately and stoically. He was incredibly healthy—I only saw him get one cold in all the years I knew and loved him. He worked hard every day of his life and helped everyone who asked him for it, and many who didn't.

One day when I was quite young I remember hearing my parents whispering about Sam Epstein. Apparently, he was gravely ill in a hospital in Baltimore, asking for his children to come to his bedside. My father was the only one who went. Mom later told us that Daddy stood by his father's bed and lovingly held his hand.

"Forgive me, son," his father whispered.

"I forgive you, Pop," is all my daddy said as his father died.

I believe with all my heart that God saw my daddy in that hospital room that day. He saw all the woundedness and hurt inside of him. And God shed a tear when my daddy extended mercy to the man who had never given it in return. Grace . . . amazing grace.

Both of my parents were born into pain and loss. But they were determined to finally have a real family—although at the time they had no idea what that actually looked like. Eventually it looked like my older brother, David; me; my baby sister, Michie; and a mutt named Zorro.

Were there hard times along the way? Way too many of them. But by the grace of God they both came to know and love their Creator and Lord and began new lives in Him. They built character in themselves and each other and then built it into their children. They never gave up even as their own bodies began to give out to age, disease, and weariness.

My father, Eppie, was diagnosed with Lewy body dementia and began an eight-year nightmare of mental and physical deterioration. He died after eight days in hospice at home on November 19, 2002. My mother had just been reciting the Twenty-Third Psalm for the umpteenth time when he suddenly lifted up, opened his eyes, let out a deep breath, and settled peacefully back onto his pillow.

Gone home . . . to his heavenly Father who had never abandoned him, never forgotten him, never disappointed him. God loved him even in his mother's unhappy womb.

Mom was a widow for the next fifteen years. Eventually we had to move her into an assisted living facility called Baywoods on the banks of the Severn River in Annapolis, where my daddy had been born and had grown into a great man.

She lived for her family's visits, Hallmark movies, and her biblical archaeological magazines. Everyone was her friend. She lit up every room she went into and stopped to talk (endlessly!) with anyone she happened to encounter in her tiny, sheltered world. She maintained her childlike love for Jesus, which had been born of great suffering. She knew Him intimately, for she knew deep in her soul that He had saved her life by sacrificing His.

Mom could no longer travel to visit my brother and me up north, so Dave and I began monthly visits to see her in Annapolis. We'd stay with our sister, Michie, near Annapolis and spend as much time with Mom as we could, talking and often taking her to her favorite restaurant, Chart House.

I lost count of the trips, but I treasure the memory of the long rides my adorable brother and I would take on the train from New York and the early morning talks with my sister, who had long ago taken on the full-time job of caretaker to our parents.

Late in August 2017, Dave and I caught the train as usual and looked forward to watching our mom delight in all the fun of having her children; her granddaughter, Shannie; Shannie's husband, Mark; and their two adorable little boys, Aaron and Zach, with her.

Unlike my daddy, Mom never lost her famous appetite. She could eat all of us under the table and feel no shame. Our last dinner together was no different. She ate her whole meal of crab cakes and moved on to everybody else's. She had a tiny sip of red wine and laughed at whatever anybody said. When we returned to Baywoods, the night nurse greeted Mom with great joy and promised she'd be in soon to give Mom her medications. It always made me sad to change Mom out of her clothes and into her nightgown, robe, and slippers. How many times had she done that for all of us when we were little? I hated leaving her there alone, although of course she wasn't there alone at all. She said she always felt her Eppie next to her and the Lord, who she knew without a doubt would never leave her side.

I settled Mom into her cozy chair and began to put on her slippers. Mom had always been beautiful, a true world-class lovely woman. But she had inherited her grandmother's feet, and by age eighty-seven, it seemed that every toe lived in a different zip code. I don't know why the sight of them this particular time broke my heart.

How does she even walk on them, Lord? I silently prayed and loved on her with all my goodbyes while fighting tears. We would always linger with her, but eventually, we had to leave.

That night I prayed, "Oh, please, Jesus, take Mommy home. Let her run on two perfect feet right into Your loving arms."

Two weeks later, God answered my prayer. Mom died peacefully in her sleep and woke up with Jesus, her Eppie, her mother, her father, her brother, her sister, and her precious grandmother who had loved her and cared for her with those incredibly painful, crippled feet. Now, Nana's feet were perfect too.

I miss my mom so much. I miss that amazing joyful smile and her contagious cackle of a laugh. I miss her being hysterically funny because she had no idea that she was hysterically funny. I love thinking about her now perfect feet and the everlasting life she has begun with her beloved Savior.

Someday it *will* be too late to kiss your mother one last time, so make the most of every opportunity you have with her. And if she's still living, call her now and maybe take her for a pedicure. One day you'll be really glad that you did.

seventeen

Make a New Friend

Give me Your strength to meet all the demands,
To reach for the hurting, please give me Your hands.
To comfort the lonely please give me Your voice
And give me Your wisdom to make the right choice.

—"ALL THAT I NEED" BY KATHIE LEE GIFFORD

In January 2016 the State of Israel requested that NBC allow me to come to the Holy Land to tape a series for Holy Week. Tourism had been suffering due to reports of terrorism in the news, and they felt that I would be able to quell some of the fears.

I have been traveling to Israel since I was seventeen. My dad gifted me a trip as my high school graduation present. Before my first trip many people said to me, "Oh, I'd love to go to Israel, but now just isn't a good time." *Any time* is a great time to visit Israel. I feel safer there than anywhere I've ever been. The Israelis are better at security than anyone. They have to be because their survival depends on it. Since they became a sovereign nation in 1948, they have been surrounded by forty million enemies who want to wipe them off the face of the earth.

NBC agreed to send me and a crew to film a five-part series that would air right before Easter, just a few weeks later. It would also be the perfect opportunity to scatter Frank's ashes over the Valley of Elah as we had decided together the year prior.

We landed at Ben Gurion Airport in Tel Aviv after a ten-hour flight. I immediately made my way to the King David Hotel in Jerusalem to prepare for our first setup at the Temple Mount just a few kilometers away inside the walls of the Old City.

Typically, I don't sleep well on these flights. Heck, I don't even sleep well in my own bed at home! But on this particular trip I also hadn't eaten much since leaving New York. I sat down for hair and makeup and then we headed for the Temple Mount, the holiest site in the Jewish faith, and one of the three holiest places in Islam.

As our crew began to set up, our very fine producer, Yael Federbush, noticed a large group of young female teenagers laughing and dancing right in front of the Western Wall, where traditionally women had been forbidden such behavior. Yael came over to me and said excitedly, "Get over there and dance with them, Kathie."

I saw the value of getting that visual, so I immediately went over and joined the girls in their celebration. To say it got out of hand is an understatement. All at once they grabbed me, pulled me into their circle, and started twirling me around—faster and faster until I feared I was going to be thrown to the ground and trampled. Just as I tried to disengage from them, one of the girls screamed into my right ear so loud, I heard something pop. My head began to pound in excruciating pain.

I stumbled away and my crew struggled to calm me and sit me down. I thought I'd maybe had a stroke or an aneurysm. I've been blessed with incredible health, energy, and stamina my whole life, but this was terrifying beyond anything that had ever happened to me. Someone handed me some acetaminophen, but it never came close to dulling the pain.

I do not know how I managed to stay upright and do my stand-up and interview there at the wall, but God got me through it. When we arrived back at the hotel where Cassidy, my daughter, was waiting for me, the pain had gotten worse, but I hoped that a ton of water and a good night's sleep would finally get me back to normal.

It was not to be. God bless Cass! She nursed me all night, but nothing helped. Finally, morning came. I got ready for the next shoot and went down to meet Yael in the lobby. The next two days were a complete blur to me: camera settings, shots, stand-ups, and interviews.

Eventually we were climbing a steep mountain to overlook the celebrated valley where David defeated Goliath. I was finally feeling better and was looking forward to reaching the summit where I could join Cody; his girlfriend, Erika; Cassidy; and my dear friend Pastor Rod VanSolkema, who was already there teaching a group that had come alongside our NBC crew to study.

I never made it. Halfway up the mountain, and halfway through filming the setup as we climbed, I felt another pop in my ears and fell to the ground with the same excruciating pain. This time it was clear I needed to get to a hospital.

Our crew car took me to Hadassah Hospital about thirty minutes away. My vision was blurred, so I kept my eyes closed, struggling in vain not to give in to the growing sense of doom so foreign to my nature. I prayed all the way there.

Yael had called ahead to arrange immediate admission. I was taken to a private room and put on a bed to await a series of tests. I was grateful to lie down, and I found myself continually looking over at the bag of Frank's ashes that I had intended to scatter in his memory at the valley. They comforted me.

The door opened and a young man entered. His name was Nurse Jihad, which, I'll admit, made me a bit uneasy. But his eyes were kind and his voice was gentle as he proceeded to take out his stethoscope and, with calmness and professionalism, begin to review my symptoms, and later direct me through the grueling set of tests that were ordered.

My twelve-hour ordeal ended with a spinal tap five thousand miles away from home but not friendless. I finished the shoot and packed for my return to New York City thinking, *This is the Israel we never hear about. This is the Israel I know and love.*

I will always be grateful for the sweet man who took care of me—a Muslim man working side by side with Jews, saving the lives of any and every person who came through their doors, including me—regardless of our race, religion, nationality, or gender.

You never know where you might meet a new friend. Keep an open mind (and heart) because they often come how and when you least expect it.

P.S. The *TODAY* show series aired as planned; we were told tourism immediately grew by 14 percent, and it has been climbing steadily ever since. I ended up scattering Frank's ashes at the Garden of Gethsemane, and I could feel him smiling.

eighteen

Go to the Holy Land

Give me Your courage to conquer my fears,
Your feet to travel the path that is narrow
To sing Your praises, the joy of the sparrow,
And faith to believe all things work for the good,
Patience to wait for the things that I should,
Grace through my troubles to persevere,
Discernment to know when temptation is near.
Give me Your eyes to see only the good.
Give me Your heart, Lord, to love as You would.

—"ALL THAT I NEED" BY KATHIE LEE GIFFORD

A motley group of both family and friends came with me on the NBC series filming trip to Israel to study rabbinically. I didn't want to take only believers, so I asked the Lord to reveal who He wanted to go. One by one they responded: a Sikh, a Hindu, Scientologists, an atheist, an agnostic, brokenhearted Catholics, and a couple of confused Baptists. Oh, yes, and two Navy SEALs! Plus my kids and Cody's girlfriend, Erika, and Frank's daughter, Vicki.

101

Really, Lord? I wondered. Our teacher, Rod VanSolkema, was going to have quite the challenge to keep all those diverse faiths and backgrounds in mind while deciphering the Scriptures in a way that illuminated truth to each individual. Our group's diversity encouraged many spirited discussions.

One by one I watched each person begin to relax and lean into Rod's teaching. Rod is not only a pastor, he's also a youth athletic coach. He is a gifted teacher with a tender, servantlike heart, and I adore him and his wife, Libby, who also teaches alongside him.

In this mean-spirited, "my way or the highway" kind of world we were becoming even then, I loved watching the Word of God wash over this special group of men and women from different cultures and faiths. They truly looked to me like the kingdom of God.

By the end of the trip it was obvious that everyone had been impacted in a life-transforming way. Clearly the power of Jesus, the Holy Land, and God's Word were profound. Later, I documented this method of study in my book *The Rock, the Road, and the Rabbi*. When you build your foundation on Truth—the Rock Himself, Jesus (Yeshua)—then walk along the very paths He walked when He became flesh and dwelt among us, then study the ancient texts of the Bible in the original source languages—Hebrew and Greek— all heaven breaks loose!

Most everyone was baptized in the Jordan River, but every single member of our insula (family) gathered together on our last morning to take communion in the Garden of Gethsemane. It was a joy to have reached a place of peace and acceptance of one another. We still stay in touch.

Watching my children being baptized in the Jordan River was one of the highlights of my life. After I left the baptism site to secure a car for a member of our group who needed assistance, I heard one final splash along with cheers from our group.

What? I thought. *What was that?* I believed everyone who wanted to had already been baptized. But I was wrong. Let me explain.

On the Wednesday after Frank died, once we had celebrated his extraordinary life in our backyard, we had a family prayer time at Praise Point—Frank's favorite place on our property.

We each took some of his ashes and had our private moments of remembrance of the beloved man we already missed. On our way back up to the house I said to Vicki, his daughter, "You need to know that your daddy died a very contented man. He was at peace. The last few years of his life, since he went to Israel, he kept saying to me, 'I'm not afraid of dying, honey. I'm actually getting really curious.'"

Vicki was understandably heartbroken and trying to process yet another devastating loss in her life. But there was one more thing I knew I had to tell her.

"Even so, there was one thing that still concerned him."

"What?" she asked.

"You, sweetie. You're his only child who still doesn't know Jesus. He wanted you to have that peace in your life too."

That next year, while on the trip to Israel, my sweet friend Anne Neilson saw Vicki sitting on a rock and sobbing as each member of our insula went into the Jordan River to be baptized.

"I want to go in there," she said through her tears, "but I don't have enough faith."

Anne's tender heart broke for her. "You've seen all the beautiful mustard seed plants everywhere?" she said.

"Yes."

"Vicki, the mustard seed starts out as the tiniest seed in all of botany. Yet nothing can destroy it once it takes hold and begins to grow. Honey, that's all you need to get you in the water. Just the faith of a mustard seed. Do you have that much?"

"Yes," she said, "I do."

After almost thirty years of sharing the hope of the Savior with her to no avail, that beautiful day at the Jordan River she surrendered to all she didn't yet understand and fell back into the arms of Pastor Rod and our dear Navy SEAL friend, Remi Adeleke.

I arrived home from Israel on a Saturday to find a message from someone at the Israeli Ministry of Tourism office in New York. Would I please meet with them on Monday to strategize for the future? *The future?* I wondered. I thought this trip had been a one-time thing, a purposeful attempt to allay the fears of visiting Israel. We had accomplished the mission, and all felt great and grateful.

After my first day back at the show, Chrissie, my longtime right-hand everything, and I sat down with them at Neary's, my favorite restaurant in New York City, to learn what was on their minds. After a few pleasantries they began to share how they wanted me to be the spokesperson for Israel for the North American continent.

"What do you mean?" I naturally countered.

"We want you to be the face of Israel in all of North America . . . to be in every square inch of our land, telling our story."

My heart leapt. I'd been praying for something like this for years.

"Gentlemen," I began, "I don't even have to pray about this!" (Impulsive? Yes. But in my exuberance I simply charged ahead.) "This is all I've wanted to do since I was twelve years old."

They were obviously pleased until I said this: "But I'm going to say something now that you've probably never heard before." I paused. "You can't pay me one penny for it. I want to be able to sit with the *New York Times* or the *Wall Street Journal* or any other publication and say honestly that I have never received a dime of compensation for performing these services. That my actions have all been completely done out of my love for God's land and His people."

They looked at each other incredulously.

I smiled at them and said, "That doesn't mean it isn't going to cost you something."

Now I had their attention.

"I want people to visit Israel—the Holy Land—and study rabbinically so that they come to an understanding of the power of God's original Word in the Greek or Hebrew."

They nodded that they understood.

"So every time I come for you to represent the State of Israel, I want you to sponsor fifty pastors or seminary students to come with me—to study alongside me. Then when they return to America, they will take with them a profound new excitement about their relationship with Yeshua and exponentially share it with others. It will cost you about three hundred thousand dollars—peanuts compared to what it would cost you to hire me through my agent." They instantly and eagerly agreed, so we spent the rest of our time together discussing the possibilities. We all left the lunch feeling excited about the future before us. Until week after week passed with little or no word from the Israeli Ministry of Tourism office. Crickets.

Our lunch meeting was in late March. Immediately afterward I had contacted the King's University in Dallas, Texas, to organize the fifty students and pastors that they deemed most deserving of a tenday, all-expense-paid rabbinical trip to Israel. They were thrilled, of course, and soon the departure day arrived—without one word from the tourism board and not one penny in the coffers to pay for their trips.

I felt I had no choice but to pay the entire amount. I couldn't disappoint all of these people whose dreams of studying in the Holy Land were about to come true. I was furious with the way things were, and very sad about the obvious miscommunication between us, but I made no mention of it publicly.

Though it was hurtful, I tried not to let bitterness take root in my heart. I convinced myself that God would use it all for good. And in time, of course, that's exactly what He did. Later, I received letters from every one of the students, who shared how blessed they had been, how they were individually affected in a positive way by the experience, and how they planned to share their education with others. This was the end that I'd hoped for and the answer to the specific prayers that I finally *did* pray.

Nothing can sour my love and enthusiasm for the Word of God as proclaimed in the original Old and New Testaments of the Bible. Nothing can diminish my love for the land and for the people—both Jewish and Palestinian—who inhabit it. And nothing will ever be able to discourage my faith in the sovereign God who sees all things and works everything for His good in spite of it.

Fifty pilgrims went to Israel that fall and came back transformed individuals. Praise His name. Don't you think maybe it's time for you to follow your own heart to the Holy Land? You know, it's never too late . . . Shalom.

nineteen

Sing Again

Yea, I am a sucker for a lovely melody,
And I respond to any song that moves me lyrically.
But singing other people's stories, 'bout other people's
    lives
Somehow, now, feels like a compromise.
And so I go to a quiet place to do what other people
    who forever have tried to do,
In a way that's all brand-new,
I try to write songs in the key of true.

—"SONGS IN THE KEY OF TRUE" BY KATHIE LEE GIFFORD
AND CHUCK HARMONY & CLAUDE KELLY OF LOUIS YORK

People come and go in our lives. Some are soon forgotten, but others make an indelible imprint. Then there are those few who are game changers, and finally, there are the life changers.

Hoda and I were scheduled to be in Nashville shooting our show during the CMA Music Festival in June 2017. I love Nashville. I'd been working there since 1978 when I filmed the ten episodes of *Hee*

Haw Honeys, but in the ensuing years I had also recorded several albums with Warner Bros. I found the people of Nashville to be great fun and truly kindhearted—good people as a whole.

For some reason I wasn't excited about this trip, but as usual, I got my game on and our producers booked a segment for the show where we were going to sit in a "writer's room" with one of the best songwriters in town and try to write a song together. They mentioned the writer, Brett James, and I said, "I've never heard of him."

"Oh, he's had over five hundred of his songs recorded. Tons of number ones."

"Like what?"

"Like 'Jesus, Take the Wheel,' 'Something in the Water . . .'" They began rattling off one huge hit after another.

I'd been songwriting for decades at this point—for theater, cabaret, jingles, you name it—but I wouldn't know a hit song if it slapped me in the face. Still, the segment sounded like fun, so at the appointed time I headed over to Brett's studio on Music Row with a short, bawdy little lyric so we'd have something to play with. Hoda was just landing at the airport, so she was going to meet us there later.

Brett and I ended up writing the song in thirty seconds, which made for a very entertaining segment for our show. As we were packing up our gear, Brett said, "Kathie, I was a big fan of your husband. I'm so sorry you lost him. How are you and your kids doing?"

"We're doing fine, Brett. Truly. I found him that morning and his face was wide with wonder. He saw Jesus, and Jesus took his breath away. And someday I'm going to write that song."

Brett didn't hesitate. "Well, then, let's write that song."

"Okay," I said, actually thinking, *Sure we will*. I wrote down my number and he said he'd call me to make a plan.

Twenty minutes later in the car my phone rang. It was Brett.

We made plans to get together the next week at his studio to write the song.

I had never sat down to write a song with someone who was pretty much a complete stranger. And since I had no idea what to expect, I wrote four lines to give us a starting point: "A little kiss. A little coffee. A little moment to pray. Our Sunday mornings always started that way."

Brett smiled. "Well, that's how we're going to start our song," he said. We finished it in all of twenty minutes and titled it "He Saw Jesus."

We spent the better part of the day talking and getting to know each other, then I headed for home. Brett flew to my house in Connecticut a couple of weeks later to record the demo in my studio. "You know I don't sing professionally anymore," I kept saying. "I damaged my vocal cords nearly fourteen years ago because of a bad case of pneumonia. My daddy was in hospice for such a short time, and I didn't want to leave and go to the doctor. I've lost thirty percent of my breathing capacity."

"Uh-huh," he said. "You'll be great. I'll protect you in the booth."

He was infuriatingly calm even as I was growing more terrified by the moment. "No, Brett, I'm serious. Who are we going to get to actually sing it?"

"We'll talk about that later," he said, nonchalantly. "Right now, let's just get your vocal down and then start working on the next song."

I struggled through the demo session. It was strange to be so insecure about a gift I had taken for granted for forty years. I'd sung on TV, in movies, in commercials, on records, on Broadway, at the White House, and at Carnegie Hall. I'd even performed at the friggin' Super Bowl! But here I was in my own home studio, nervous as a newbie on a tightwire.

An hour later Brett was convinced we had a great demo of "He Saw Jesus," so we wrapped our session and went upstairs to start a brand-new song that eventually became "Once Again." (This ended up being the first of seven songs that we would collaborate on for the *Then Came You* movie soundtrack.)

It was a very creative time for me—something I realized was both healing and energizing as I stepped into the next phase of my life. It was actually one week earlier that Brett had seen a script in my bag and asked me what I was working on.

"Oh, it's this movie I'm writing for my friend Craig Ferguson."

"I love that guy! I miss him on late-night," he said.

"Yeah, he's brilliant," I agreed.

"Can I look?"

"Of course."

A few minutes later Brett said, "Kathie, these lyrics are gorgeous! Let's write this next."

This is how crazy my life had become. I had done a fifteen-minute segment for the *TODAY* show with a total stranger, we wrote a tremendously personal song together about finding my dead husband on the floor, and the next thing I knew I was writing seven songs for a feature film with one of the greatest songwriters in the business.

The next morning I was getting ready to leave for the studio in New York and Brett was leaving to go back to Nashville. I took a cup of coffee over to his guest suite to say goodbye and he said, "You did a great job on the demo, Kath."

"Really? You'll fix all my croaks and clams?"

"Yeah, I'm gonna comp [create a composite of best takes] your vocals, give 'em to Sal, a great producer and engineer, and we're gonna add some live strings."

That was a dead giveaway of what he was up to: you never add live strings to a demo. I glared at him. "You bamboozled me!"

He shrugged and laughed it off. "Only Kathie Lee Gifford can sing this song. And it's gonna change the world," he said.

Well, it certainly changed mine. A few months later I sang "He Saw Jesus" on the *TODAY* show and had my very first number-one song on iTunes. It stayed on the top of the gospel chart for a long time. In response, Brett and I donated our royalties to Samaritan's Purse to help out the victims of Hurricane Maria.

Our collaboration continued and we wrote "Jesus Is His Name" and performed it together at the White House Christmas tree lighting for a Hallmark TV special. Boom! Second number-one hit on iTunes, only to be followed a couple of months later with our third number-one song, "Love Me to Death," from our movie of the same name at the time.

I was stunned and asked Brett, "Is this normal?"

"No," he said with a laugh. "I wish."

Months later Brett and his daughter, Clare, spent the weekend in New York going to two Tony Award–winning musicals. Afterward they came to visit me in my home in Connecticut. Brett asked if he could hear some of the score to the Broadway musical *Scandalous* that I had written many years prior. My heart stopped. I hadn't been able to listen to a note of the cast album since the show had closed more than four years earlier. It was still too painful.

Scandalous, which first ran under the title *Saving Aimee*, is the story of the life and career of evangelist and pop-culture icon Aimee Semple McPherson. The music was written with David Pomeranz, David Friedman, and me, and featured songs such as "Stand Up!," "I Have a Fire," and "For Such a Time as This." Carolee Carmello, the extraordinary and brilliant leading lady, went on to receive a Tony Award nomination for Best Leading Actress in a Musical for her portrayal of McPherson. She gave the finest performance I have ever seen by any Broadway actress. When she was nominated, we felt like we all were.

"I guess I could play you one song," I told Brett, though I was not sure I actually could.

"No, I want to hear the whole thing."

I gulped and went to find the CD. Minutes later, over dinner in my garden, I watched them as they listened. Clare was seventeen years old at the time—the exact age that Aimee is when the musical begins. By the third song Clare said, "Daddy, this is so much better than anything we saw this weekend."

"It is, honey," he agreed.

My heart soared.

After five songs Brett put down his fork, leaned back in his chair, and closed his eyes. When he opened them, he looked at me and said, "You wrote this? Every word?"

"Yes," I told him honestly, "and forty more songs that didn't make the cut."

He responded by saying one word, and in doing so, gave me the single greatest compliment I have ever been paid in my entire career. I won't share it here because it's too embarrassing, but believe me when I tell you, it changed my entire perspective on the incredibly agonizing Broadway experience. Once again I found the gift of closure, like when Brett and I wrote and recorded "He Saw Jesus." This time it was closure from all of the pain I had experienced during the thirteen years it took to write and produce *Scandalous*.

What memories have you locked away that are too painful to share? Sometimes God heals you in the blink of an eye; more often it seems to take forever. The beauty in the long road is that He will often use someone else to be a part of your healing. And who knows—this someone might even bamboozle you into singing again. Thank you, Brett.

twenty
Commiserate with
Sting in a Stairway

I didn't choose this journey I'm on.
This journey was chosen for me.
I didn't ask for this task I've been given,
And I'd give it up, gratefully.
If I could
I would.
But I won't.
I can't.
All of the broken lives, and all of the broken dreams
Coming down the aisles in steady streams.

—"FOR SUCH A TIME AS THIS" BY KATHIE
LEE GIFFORD FROM *SCANDALOUS*

I have experienced both triumph and tragedy on Broadway. Though I was thrilled to step in for Carol Burnett and perform in *Putting It Together*, *Scandalous* was devastating for me. It remains the single biggest disappointment in my professional life. It's still difficult for me to pass the Neil Simon Theatre on West Fifty-Second Street. It's painful to look up at the marquis and see a different name of a show.

I avoided the theater as long as I could until Sting asked me to attend a performance of his new musical called *The Last Ship*—a poignant story about the failing shipbuilding industry in England. I have always adored Sting and admired his music enormously. He's a true musical artist of the highest order and a very sweet man.

I had heard that the show was in trouble. Even a star as big as Sting was having difficulty at the box office; the critics had not been kind (that's news?), and there was talk of it actually closing. I sat in the theater waiting for the curtain to rise. I totally understood everything he was going through. My heart was breaking for him as I watched his sensational cast perform his artfully crafted songs. At the end of the show the performers received a rousing standing ovation.

People who have never written, produced, and performed, and critics who couldn't do these things if they tried, have no idea how difficult and all-consuming the work is. There's an old Broadway saying often attributed to Larry Gelbart: "If Hitler is alive, I hope he's out of town with a musical." It's funny but true. The musical theater process is brutal from beginning to end, and few shows ever turn a profit, much less become a bona fide hit.

I really enjoyed *The Last Ship* and was looking forward to meeting with Sting afterward to tell him so. For some reason he had asked me to meet him in the stairwell outside of the main dressing room. I knew the area well as I had spent many a moment there with Carolee during *Scandalous*.

Sting arrived and sat down on the stairs. It was another one of those surreal moments in my life. I had seen him onstage at Lincoln Center and had been with him on my television shows, at the GRAMMYs, and at celebrity parties in New York. But I never would have dreamed that I'd be sitting on the stairs with him in this musty, dusty, decrepit staircase of a theater that has only been home to one real hit: *Hairspray*.

Sting is a magnificently handsome, magnetic man. But on this day he seemed weary, and I ached with recognition. Our conversation went something like this.

"I don't understand, Kathie Lee," he started. "I understand the world *out there* [outside of Broadway], but I don't understand this one. It makes no sense. Show after show I watch the audience. They're involved, they're laughing, they're crying, they're standing up and cheering in the end." He shook his head. "I don't understand."

"I know, Sting." I nodded. It was the same way with *Scandalous*. "It's like the critics watch a completely different show than real people do."

"I'm thinking about going into the show myself for a while. To try to save it."

"That's what I was planning to do when mine closed. We just ran out of time."

It seems some dreams are like that. No matter what you do, or how hard you work, they sometimes simply run themselves right out of time to become what you had imagined they would be. It's true for all of us—even for music icons like Sting or crazy creatives like me.

Still, dead ends don't have to be the end of dreaming. And they're certainly not the end of opportunities that lie ahead. But perhaps they provide a unique opportunity to commiserate with a friend . . . even one named Sting.

twenty-one
Have a Party

We looked at one another so many years ago
And found something special in our eyes.
We vowed to each other
There would never be another.
For if love is truly real, then love never dies.

—"OUR LOVING EYES" BY KATHIE LEE GIFFORD

The world's loss on February 21, 2018, was heaven's gain. That was the day Billy Graham left this world at the age of ninety-nine to enter into his greatest eternal adventure. I was sitting in the makeup chair at NBC that morning when the news came over the wires. I immediately raised my face and lifted my arms to the skies and said, "Thank You, Jesus."

I had known Billy since I was in my early twenties and had been immeasurably blessed to be counted among his friends. He and my daddy were both the finest men I had ever been privileged to know, and now he was home, just like my daddy was—finally in the arms of the Savior he had so willingly and faithfully served for many decades. I rejoiced for him.

The last time I had seen him was at his ninety-fifth birthday in Asheville, North Carolina.

He was extremely frail, and I feared that all the excitement of the evening would be too much for him. Billy had always hated being the center of attention. All he ever wanted was for his God to be glorified.

I sat one table away and watched him as person after person gave testimony of Billy's extraordinary influence on their lives. I truly believe that no one in history has ever personally been responsible for so many millions of people coming to faith in Jesus.

My mind went back to 1996 when Frank and I had attended the ceremony at the Capitol where Billy and his magnificent wife, Ruth, both received a Congressional Gold Medal—the highest honor the government can give a civilian. We loved sharing this moment with them. Ruth was extremely ill at the time and sat in a wheelchair next to the podium, never speaking, as again, person after person rose up to exalt the honorees.

When it had been Billy's turn to address the audience assembled in that esteemed and time-honored place in history, there was not a sound to be heard. He looked around at the busts of treasured heroes featured in the rotunda and gestured for us to see and consider them too.

"They have one thing in common: they're all dead. And we're going to join them. . . . If ever we needed God's help, it is now. If ever we needed spiritual renewal, it is now. And it can begin today in each one of our lives as we repent before God and yield ourselves to Him and His Word. What are you as an individual going to do?"[4]

Frank and I then left to go to our hotel and get ready for the reception. I turned the television on and caught a CNN reporter saying, "Today in Washington, DC, Billy Graham received the Congressional Gold Medal . . ."

"So did Ruth!" I literally screamed at the television. "So did Ruth!" I was furious. Billy had said innumerable times that he *never* would have been able to travel the world, crusade after crusade, if his beloved wife, Ruth, had not been *equally called* to stay at Montreat and take care of the home and family he loved so much.

I sighed with the memory and looked over again at my precious ninety-five-year-old friend. *Oh, Lord*, I thought, *he looks so tired, so weary. Please, Lord, let the evening end and give him the rest he so longs for.* Finally, as the party was coming to a close, I leaned over to Billy's granddaughter, Courtney, sitting next to me.

"Sweetie," I whispered, "do you think it would be okay if I go over and say goodbye?"

"Of course, Kathie," she said, "he would love that."

I doubted he would even know that I was there, but I just knew I had to go. I was never going to see him in this life again, I was sure. I quietly walked over to his wheelchair and stooped down so I could look into his beloved face. He was leaned over and still.

"Billy, Billy," I said softly. "It's Kathie Lee. I have to thank you one last time for all you have meant to me and my family."

Billy raised his head up slowly and I watched as he struggled to focus his blue eyes on the face before his. "Oh, Kathie Lee, I love you."

My heart burst as I embraced this lion of the faith with my last goodbye. I didn't want him to see my tears. I saved them for later when only God could see.

Mere moments after the announcement of Billy's death, the phone rang in the makeup room. I'd known it would. Journalists always want to talk to people who knew the deceased personally. There would be plenty of air to fill later for people with opinions but no relationship.

The call was from the senior producer of *Megyn Kelly Today*, which was about to begin taping across the street from our studio.

Megyn knew of my friendship with Billy. I had called to take her to lunch on six Thursdays in a row a few months before. I had hoped to help her navigate the inevitable ugly tabloid waters that come with entering into daytime television.

During our lunches I had shared my faith with her and the strength I had received from it when it was my turn to "be in the barrel," as Frank called it. I know she appreciated our time together because she told me so. And I knew she would want me on her show to talk about the man I knew and loved, not the legend the world thought they knew.

I sat down across from Megyn in the studio aware once again that millions of eyes would be waiting to see, and millions of ears would be waiting to hear—what? I had no idea. So, I chose to share what I always want to know—the truth.

I talked about coming to faith in Jesus in a movie theater when I was twelve years old while watching the Billy Graham film *The Restless Ones*. I talked about him coming to my house in Connecticut in November 1994 to tape my Christmas special and wanting a Big Mac.

He was also the first person to call me when I was falsely accused of operating sweatshops and after it was revealed that Frank had cheated on me and broken my heart.

"Oh, Kathie, honey," he'd always begin, "how are you doin'?"

Then he would tell me again how much Jesus loved me and how He was going to get me through this and make all things new. And, often, he'd ask, "May I please talk to Frank too?"

I remember the look on Frank's face when I passed the phone to him after the news of the infidelity broke. I watched as Billy's words of mercy and grace washed over him. I could see his eyes well up with tears as he heard Billy's magnificent voice tell him, "Remember, Frank, there is now no condemnation in Christ. We all have sinned and fallen short of the glory of God."

"Thank you, Billy," was all Frank could say.

So, I'll say it again for all of us:

Thank you, Billy Graham. Thank you. Forever.

I wrote a song with Phil Sillas for Billy and Ruth to celebrate their extraordinary marriage, which lasted over sixty years. "Our Loving Eyes" tells the story of a legacy of living through the ups and downs of life together and ends with this picture of their beautiful, extraordinary love:

No need to speak of all we share.
It comes as no surprise
That we'll continue our sweet romance
With our eyes, our loving eyes.

No need to speak of all we feel.
We know what's true, we know what's real.
And until we whisper the last of our last goodbyes
We'll continue our romance
With our loving eyes.

We dreamed our dreams together, we walked the narrow road,
Shared every burden side by side.
And as we turned each corner, we turned to God above,
Depending on His grace to sanctify our love.

Now we sit by the fire,
Weathered by the years,
Strengthened by the trials,
Tendered by the tears.

When Billy's casket was lying in state at the rotunda on February 28, 2018, the president walked up to pay his respects. He solemnly reached out to touch the casket to say goodbye. And the song they were playing through the Capitol speakers that very moment? That special gift from God and Brett James. "He saw Jesus. He saw Jesus. And He took his breath away."

twenty-two
Write a Movie

What is life but a movie?
You film one frame at a time,
From the ways that you grow to the places you go,
From the meadows you cross to the mountains you
    climb.
Everyone writes their own movie, and no one
    knows how it will end.
But we can spend each and every new day
Trying to find a brand-new way to say
To the one who's become your best friend:
I love you, I do.
And the miracle of my life is you love me too.
And in this crazy world all around us
Love came and actually found us . . .
Once again.

—"ONCE AGAIN" BY KATHIE LEE GIFFORD

FROM *THEN CAME YOU*

I was thrilled when Hoda called me one day to give me the wonderful news that she had adopted a baby girl and was going on maternity leave immediately. I wasn't thrilled with the idea of a new cohost every day, but I was so happy for her that I was determined to make the best of it.

We were several shows in when I learned that Craig Ferguson had been booked to cohost with me for one day. Nothing could have prepared me for what happened next.

I'd met Craig years before when I guest-hosted on *The Drew Carey Show*. He was a regular on that series, and I liked him immediately. He's impossible not to like, and his Scottish accent is nothing short of enchanting. (Yes, that is the word I choose to use because it's true!)

The day arrived and so did Craig. He is one of those rare performers—much like a Robin Williams or Ricky Gervais—who simply commands a room instantly. In a good way. He charmed the crew and had everyone laughing and happy in mere moments. You instantly knew you'd better buckle up because this guy was going to take you on a ride. A very bumpy ride.

The show was a thrilling mixture of terror, hilarity, sexiness, and insanity, and I fell in love with the extraordinary spontaneity and organic humanity of it. I wanted more.

"Please, Tammy," I begged our executive producer, "you've got to get him back here next week. He's unbelievable!"

She agreed. And the crazy Scot showed up the next Monday for four more riotous days. We had to put a ten-second delay on the show because it was so out of control and everyone was petrified we'd get pulled off the air.

I had had an amazing fifteen-year run with Regis, and an equally amazing but different eleven-year run with Hoda, but the five days I spent hosting with Craig were mind-blowing. The constant energy, the unpredictability, the side-splitting hysteria were all things I'd never experienced. At the end of the week he suggested we have lunch before we parted ways.

"You know, Kath, if we wait for our f–ing agents to get us a job on TV, we're going to die waiting."

"I know," I agreed.

"Let's write a movie together," he suggested.

I agreed.

Craig left New York with his wife, Megan, and son, Liam, and boarded a flight for Los Angeles. I returned to Connecticut full of creative joy and promptly fell asleep from the kind of exhaustion you can only experience when you have been with a whackadoodle whirlwind for a week.

At two o'clock the next morning I woke up knowing just what our movie should be. I got out of bed, took the dogs out, poured the coffee, and started writing my brains out! I didn't stop until noon when I called Craig.

"Hi, Craig, it's Kath."

"Yes, Kath?" I could tell he was confused.

"Uh . . . you know that movie we talked about? That we were going to write together?"

"Yes," he said.

I swallowed. "I think I just wrote it."

"What?" he responded. "I've barely landed my Scottish ass home."

"I know," I said. "I'm sorry. But it came to me just a few hours after you left, and I've been writing ever since. I've written six scenes. Can I send them to you?"

"Of course," he answered. "Send them, and I'll call you tomorrow."

"Okay," I said excitedly and sent them.

The next day Craig called. "Kathie, this is your baby. I stand ready to serve."

I think my scream of joy must have been heard in the Highlands. The ensuing months were a blur. Writing, rewriting, calling investors, rewriting again, flying to Nashville to write the songs, recording the songs, shooting the videos of the songs . . . all of it. There was only one snag—we were scheduled to shoot in June, and we had *not one penny* invested by February. I needed $5.7 million or it wasn't going to happen. Movies are incredibly risky crapshoots. Only fools or insanely wealthy people tend to be willing to invest in them.

I became increasingly agitated and nervous as the deadline approached to guarantee the crew, the locations, the cast, and the travel so that the Scottish tax credits were reached in order to afford to film (a common practice in the film industry to entice producers to film in their area). I was staying with my friend Anne Neilson in her home in Charlotte, doing a book tour for *The Rock, the Road, and the Rabbi*. We had reached the end of the line. We needed a miracle.

Five of us got on our faces in the Neilsons' living room that day to pray. I was ready to give up, but as we all got up from the floor I said, "Is there a name that any of you can think of—someone who might be interested in our movie at this late date? Anyone?"

Immediately another friend, Anne Ferrell Tata, cried out, "George Shinn."

"Who?" we all asked simultaneously.

"George Shinn. He's a scoundrel, but he's a wonderful man, and he loves Jesus and loves the arts."

Well, I love Jesus, too, and Jesus loved scoundrels, so I said, "Call him, please!"

And she did. It was about eight thirty in the morning, but George responded immediately and said, "Have Kathie call me."

I said a silent prayer and called him right away. I think we had a twenty-minute conversation about the movie. (He later said, "No, it was ten.") He could not have been more lovable. In his sweet North Carolina accent he said, "Well, Kathie Lee, now you got me all fired up! But I don't do anything without my money man, Spencer. I'll call him and you two can talk about it."

I couldn't believe my ears. My heart was pounding. "Okay, George, thank you so much, but I'm about to head to the airport to catch a flight."

"Where are ya going?" he asked.

"Palm Beach. I'm on a book tour."

"Well, that's where Spencer is," he said with a laugh. "I'll have him call you, and you two can get together."

Which is exactly what we did. The next day. And against all odds and anything that makes sense in a real world, George Shinn agreed to executive produce a movie he had never read by a woman he had never met to be shot in four months in a place he'd never been to.

This story is God's truth and proof that it's not only never too late to pray about everything but also never too late to trust God to provide everything you need. And though you may not have written a movie or be needing to finance it, I'm sure there are things you've gone after that could be identified as "more than you can chew." If so, consider this your nudge to do what I did—stop, drop, and pray.

twenty-three
Change the Ending,
Then Change It Again

So many years I sat in the shadows,
Only flickering embers around me,
Believing the darkness would never end.
Music would never surround me again.
And beauty would never astound me again.
Then came you.
Then came you.

—"THEN CAME YOU" BY KATHIE LEE GIFFORD

I arrived in Glasgow at the end of May 2018, jet-lagged but excited, and went directly to our production office to meet up with the film's leading man, Craig Ferguson, and the director, Adriana Trigiani. I was also scheduled to have wardrobe fittings with the costume designer, Michael Herz. I jumped into Craig's arms because I was so happy to see him.

I sensed a little tension when I joined up with Craig and Adriana but couldn't imagine what was causing it. I mean, I adored these two people. What could be wrong? I wasn't there five minutes when Craig said, "Kathie, you know I love you, and you know I love the script . . . or I wouldn't be here, right?"

"Yeah?" I waited what seemed like forever as Craig and Adriana exchanged a look.

"You've got to change the ending," Craig said directly. "You can't be in a coma with me moping all around you."

"What?" I practically screamed. "We start shooting in two days!"

"I know," he said, "but hear me out. I have an idea."

I wanted to cry. I hadn't slept on the plane during the flight from New York to Heathrow, then had missed my connection to Glasgow. I was exhausted and hungry and now, I've gotta admit, a little upset that no one had discussed this with me before I arrived.

Craig immediately said, "Listen, I know this is the last thing a writer wants to hear, but would you please let me tell you what I'm thinking before you say no?"

I had no choice. "Okay, but what if I hate it?"

He chuckled. "You won't. Cause you want what's best for this film just like I do, and you're going to agree that it's a better idea."

"If it's better than my idea, then of course we'll change it," I said. "And I'll take all the credit."

"Okay, good." Craig seemed relieved and proceeded to completely change *the entire scene.*

I looked at Adriana. "What do you think, Adriana? Do you agree?"

"Yes," she said. "I think it's better. It's something we've never seen in a movie before."

"That's for sure . . . okay," I finally agreed. "But if it sucks, I'm going to blame you both!"

We all laughed, and I tried to start breathing normally again. I had spent a year writing this movie, and in one minute my favorite part was gone and replaced with something that was going to either ruin the whole thing or work so brilliantly it would have the audience completely speechless.

Then I think I said, "Why the hell didn't I hire Pierce Brosnan?"

Finally, after three hours in fittings (which I hate), my darling assistant, Alysia, drove me up to what would be my home in the glorious Scottish Highlands for the next six weeks. She drove right past the hotel where the crew was staying and stopped directly in front of an ugly trailer in an equally ugly trailer park.

"What are we doing here?" I asked.

"This is where you're staying. It's got four bedrooms, a fireplace, and a hot tub."

I couldn't believe it. Every window looked out onto, you guessed it, another trailer. The gorgeous nearby loch was completely out of sight. I swore I could hear it laughing at me. "Hey there, Miss Big-Shot Movie Star. Oh, you're the writer too? And the executive producer? Ha! So sad!"

"But nobody's coming to stay with me, and it's one hundred degrees outside. Why would I want a fireplace and a hot tub in June?"

I wasn't being mean to her, I promise. I was just stunned that anyone would think this was a good idea.

"Alysia, please understand, I'll be working fourteen-hour days on set and then doing rewrites at night. I feel like I need to be in some place that at least feeds my soul, or I'm going to be a disaster, and it's going to ruin the whole experience for me and everybody."

Alysia was sweet and unflappable. In her crisp British accent, she said, "Yes, well, I completely agree, of course. This actually is a dreary mishmash of a mess, isn't it? Let me make a call."

I had liked her before. Now I wanted to kiss her feet.

"Thank you so much," I said, relieved.

I'm only telling this part of the story because it's important to how the story ends. And know that I am a lot of bad things (ask my children), but I'm not a diva. I have stayed in many a hellhole, done my hair and makeup in gas station bathrooms, and eaten inedible slop on location. But there was too much riding on this project, and I had to safeguard my health and my sanity for everyone's sake. I moved into the hotel.

The next day a miracle happened. Two close friends of mine from America were visiting and "just happened" to be driving along Loch Goil when they came upon the most charming little lodge nestled along the shore. The gate, which I learned later was *never* left open, was open. They drove down the steep driveway and parked at the front door of the lodge. They were immediately greeted by the owner, a charming Scot named Iain Hopkins, who explained that while they had never been closed in June, they were presently closed because of a family matter. My friends promised Iain that I wouldn't be much trouble at all, didn't eat much, and would be really low maintenance.

These were my two Annes—Anne Neilson from Charlotte and Anne Ferrell Tata from Virginia Beach. These women finagled my scrawny self a six-week stay at the most beautiful spot in the most beautiful lodge in all of the Highlands. It truly was a miracle! As I unpacked in my room I caught glimpses of the loch, maybe one hundred yards away. It wasn't laughing at me anymore. It was singing and whistling and calling to me.

"Hey, you up there, unpacking your underwear! Get a good night's sleep. Anybody crazy enough to think they can pull off an independent film while wearing six hats and no SPANX deserves a proper Scottish welcome."

At the bottom of the lodge's steep driveway was something that had caught my eye the moment we drove up. (I can't tell you exactly what it is because I'm hoping the movie is finally going to come out sometime before I die, and I don't want to spoil the surprise for you.) Suffice it to say it is used for tiny weddings and five-star fine dining. It soon became my favorite spot on the property. On many nights Iain would host dinners for me and my producers, guests, or Craig and our guest stars, like Elizabeth Hurley. Iain was truly the loveliest, warmest host. He and his partner, Alice, and their son, Luke, made us all feel like family. As I sat there night after night I couldn't stop thinking, *How can I get this place in the movie? How?*

I had one day off a week, so I always tried to make it special. When the weather was gorgeous, which it often was, I would take long hikes in the glorious Highlands. I fell in love with Scotland—its history, its people, its music, and its rhythm of life.

One Saturday, with only two weeks of shooting left, I went on a five-hour "sing at the top of your lungs like Maria in *The Sound of Music*" praise hike. It was the mother of all hikes. I wish I could describe the beauty of it. And I wish you could breathe in the freshness of the hills and the loch and the flowers. There is a lilt in the land in the Highlands that makes the heart joyful.

Finally, I sensed the Lord saying very clearly, "Go home, Kathie. Go to your spot, take your pen and paper, and meet Me there. I have a surprise for you."

As I've told you, I've learned to be quick to obey that voice as soon as I hear it. So, I did exactly as He said.

Iain must have seen me come back because he followed me, bearing a bottle of GIFFT wine and a goblet. (Yes, I had it shipped there. No judgment, please!) He quietly opened the shutters out to the loch as the sun was setting. Then he lit the charming corner fireplace and left me without making a sound, though I could feel him smiling.

In the stillness and sweetness of that beloved spot, I began to receive the gift God had for me.

The lyrics flowed effortlessly, and I marveled at the tender way God longs to bless His children. All we have to do is listen for His voice and grow still in His presence.

And then I knew. I was supposed to change the ending of the movie yet again and change the name of the film from *Love Me to Death* to *Then Came You*, which was also the name of the song I'd just written.

"That's crazy!" Adriana yelled into the phone. "You can't change the title or the ending this late in a shoot."

"You come over here and see what I see and then you tell me who's crazy."

Then I climbed down the stairs and called Brett and read him the lyrics.

"Oh my God, Kath," is all I remember him saying.

Two days later Brett sent me the finished song, and it was my turn to say, "Oh my God, Brett. It's gorgeous."

God is full of surprises. Sometimes He surprises us with the brand-new way a story reveals itself, which can inspire us to new heights of creativity—that is, if we're not afraid to go there and not afraid of what anyone will think. Breathe some rare fresh air. It's never too late.

twenty-four
Stop Yelling

Some people long for a crystal ball
To see what lies before them.
Others seek psychics to speak to the spirits
Tho, I am inclined to ignore them.
Why do we hunger to know today
What only tomorrow knows?
Why can't we live in this moment, right now
And see how the next moment goes?
Because we are afraid.

—"AFRAID" BY KATHIE LEE GIFFORD

Even though it's been twenty years since I left *Live with Regis and Kathie Lee*, I still get asked about Regis almost every day. "How is he? Is he okay? What's he doing? Do you see him? Are you still friends?"

I'm always delighted to answer: "He's great! Living in California most of the time now to be close to his family. I try to see him whenever I can. We'll be friends until the day we die."

People still love him so much. He was an incredible part of the American landscape for more than five decades and a true pioneer in the television industry. People also ask, "What was the secret to your success?" We always had the same answer: "Fun." Simple as that. There was not a scripted moment. We had no writers—everything was spontaneous and real. And I'm certain that is why it lasted as long and as successfully as it did. We were authentic. Love us or loathe us, viewers knew they were getting the real deal.

So much of our culture today is manipulated, photoshopped, and edited into sound bites. Over the years I've been asked to participate in reality shows, but I've always said no because they aren't "reality" at all. They are planned and produced and manipulated to titillate and entertain to the lowest common denominator, which usually includes some form of human degradation. I simply *cannot* watch people be devalued in any way, let alone participate in a show that promotes this.

A part of our not being respectful of each other's humanity includes the fact that people no longer talk to each other; they scream at each other. Our dialogue has become coarse and mean-spirited. I've had to move away from this culture of hate to a culture of kindness.

What goes in must come out, right?

I'm glad I'm not on live daily television anymore, walking on political eggshells and dodging proverbial bullets. It's no fun. I'm not sure *Live with Regis and Kathie Lee* could have lasted in this social media–dominated world we live in now. We always just said whatever came to our minds. Now you have to process every thought and edit every word before you feel safe enough to actually say it. The result: no spontaneity and little authenticity. In other words, no fun.

It makes me sad for young people growing up today. How can you *find* yourself if you're not allowed to *be* yourself?

My two favorite comedians in the world are Craig Ferguson and Ricky Gervais. They are true comic geniuses who happen to be delightful human beings as well. They are explosive but deeply insightful men who remain my friends even though, in many ways, we are polar opposites.

One day Craig and I were taking a break on the set of our movie and he asked suddenly, "Kathie, why do you love me and Ricky?"

"What?" I said. "What do you mean, 'why do I love you?' I love you because you're wonderful and hysterical and I adore being around you."

"But we're not good guys!" he exclaimed. "We don't agree with you on hardly anything."

"So?" I answered him. "God loves you, and I love God, so I love who He loves."

Then Craig told me something that tore at my soul. "Nobody of faith has ever told us before that they love us."

"Well, then you haven't met one. Any person who truly loves God truly loves the people He has created. You can't proclaim that you love God when you actually hate someone."

And then we got back to work—two very different people with very different ideas about pretty much everything who had been blessed to find each other in a screwed-up world yet were completely unwilling to let it screw *us* up.

It's never too late to politely ask others to stop yelling. Then as much as it depends on you, have a civil conversation. I'm right here. You don't have to yell.

twenty-five
Discover a Godwink

We all get used to the way things are,
The rising sun and the falling star,
Each day the same as the day before,
Rarely noticing anything more.
But then all at once the winds can turn,
Leaving us with new lessons to learn.
Oh, there will be problems as we travel on,
And there will be mountains to climb.
But it's always darkest before the dawn,
And morning always shows up right on time.
Morning always shows up right on time.

—"MORNING" BY KATHIE LEE GIFFORD

I have two very dear friends known separately as SQuire and Louise but now known as SQuise in my family. Louise DuArt has always been an entertainer and comedian. SQuire Rushnell was an executive at *Good Morning America* in the '70s and '80s but in recent years has become a highly successful producer and author of a series of books called Godwinks. The books contain true stories of peoples' experiences with what appear initially to be coincidences but in reality are moments in time when the divine aligns with the human. When God is "winking" in our lives. Interestingly, in the Hebrew language there is no word for "coincidence" because there is no such thing. Sovereign God is either truly sovereign in all things or not God at all.

Several years ago, we began featuring these Godwink stories on *TODAY*. They were highly rated segments, so SQuise and I took the concept to Hallmark.

It took three years to get our deal done. Initially there was concern that an audience would be offended by the faith element, but I knew there was potentially a huge viewership just dying for wholesome, true, faith-based movies that gave them hope. We convinced Hallmark to try one and find out.

SQuise and I filmed the first movie, *A Godwink Christmas*, in Vancouver. It is based on the romantic love story of the real inn owners of the Charlotte Inn, located on the elegant island of Martha's Vineyard. My character was the determined aunt from the neighboring island of Nantucket who is right in the thick of getting the couple together. (It was fun taking my acting chops out of the mothballs again!) The movie was top-rated for the network and was voted by fans as their favorite inspirational Hallmark movie of the 2018 holiday season.

In 2019 we filmed *A Godwink Christmas: Meant for Love*. In this inspiring true story an amazing Godwink brought together a sweet couple, Alice and Jack, who both had given up on love. As Alice's mom, Olga, my character was the encouraging yet feisty matriarch, right in the middle of it all. IMDb called the film one of the ten best Hallmark movies of the last decade—again setting record ratings. We're currently writing our third Hallmark script, *A Godwink*

Christmas: Second Chances, and are hoping to start making these films year-round, not just for Christmas.

Before our films released, we'd been told that the word *God* had never before in television history been used in the title of any movie. Besides making great movies we were also making a little history!

SQuise and I are grateful that God would wink at us with these stories and opportunities. It's been a Godwink to work with them but also to discover a brand-new audience waiting to be found.

twenty-six

Meet an Angel

I'm gonna make a clean start,
Wash the cold winter away,
Put a scrubby dubby spring in my heart,
And cart the old garbage away . . . Allez!
So what if I get soap suds in my ears?
So what if I get soapy suds in my eyes?
This is the most fun I've had in years.
Out of the ashes the phoenix will rise.

—"I'M GOING TO MAKE A CLEAN START" BY KATHIE
LEE GIFFORD, FROM *UNDER THE BRIDGE*

Several years ago Cody introduced me to an extraordinary woman named Angie Clawson. She is basically the heart and soul of the Nashville chapter of an organization called "I Am Second." You cannot miss Angie. Born of Mexican heritage, her magnificent hair enters a room before she does. And her smile and laugh will melt you. Everyone adores her.

Angie is married to a funny, sweet soul named Greg McCollum.

When I met them I had no idea that a few years later, when I moved to Nashville, they would become so important to me. But they certainly did.

As far as it goes for Angie and me, think Lucy and Ethel. Or maybe Thelma and Louise. You get the picture. We have become inseparable, and I hate when I have to leave town, knowing I'm gonna miss my Angie so much. It is a genuine sisterhood. I'm deeply grateful to her and Greg for being there for me at every turn during my life transition to Tennessee.

We all desperately need angels in our lives—ethereal beings who show up "out of the blue" to bless, caress, and direct us. Especially in the deep state of loneliness I was in when I arrived in town. Angie and Greg dragged me everywhere: music festivals, clubs, church, parades (which I hate), restaurants, dinners, lunches. You name it, they dragged me there.

And something magical happened. I had fun. The show with Hoda had been fun, of course, but I hadn't had fun in my personal life for several years—actually the four years since Frank had passed. I hardly ever went out. Now I was out someplace almost every night. Or they'd be at my house just hanging out and sharing life. It's almost as if they were afraid to leave me alone. They understood my deep sense of loss and my desire to belong again, to be surrounded by sweet, like-minded souls who laugh or cry with you one minute and get down on their knees and pray for you the next.

They get me.

What happened in July 2019 is a prime example. I had just moved into my larger townhouse when Angie called to tell me about a new fitness company called Manduu. I've always been disciplined about exercising but never liked it and certainly didn't love it as so many people do. I'd never experienced that endorphin rush they talk about. Honestly, the best part of any workout for me was when it was over.

Because Angie asked and agreed to go to a Manduu studio with me, I said yes. I saw a difference almost immediately. But what surprised me most was that I started sleeping better, had tons more energy, and began looking visibly more muscular.

In November of that year I returned to the *TODAY* show for the first time since I'd left to promote *A Godwink Christmas: Meant for Love.* I was sitting in the hair and makeup room getting ready for the show when Jenna Bush Hager came in.

"Kathie Lee!" she screamed. "What have you done to yourself?"

"What are you talking about?" I thought she maybe meant my new blonde highlights.

"*Hell* no," she roared, going all Texas woman on me. "Look at your guns!"

"What guns?" I truly did not know what she meant.

"These guns." She came over and squeezed my biceps. "Girl, where did you get these?"

I laughed and then tried to explain to her about my new exercise program.

"Well, you've gotta show Hoda your arms on the air," she insisted.

"I'm not gonna show Hoda!" I laughed. "I'll show her after the show."

Jenna is a rascal, and yep, right there live on the air, while I was trying to promote my movie, she yelled for me to show Hoda my arms.

There was no way those women were going to let this get by them, and I knew it. So I took off the sweater I was wearing and made a muscle for Hoda. She gasped. The crew gasped. I laughed. I had left *TODAY* a scrawny 108 pounds seven months before, and now they were acting like I was Wonder Woman. Thanks, Angie!

Angie was instrumental in my life in many ways. Years before she had been married to a top songwriter in Nashville and was still friendly with pretty much everybody in the business. She began setting up "writes" for me before I even made my move to Nashville—basically a session where songwriters get together in a room for the express purpose of writing a song.

These writes have been fascinating for me. I must have had fifty of them the first full year I was in town. Each one is completely different because the people are all so different. I love these sessions and look forward to them.

Have I had a hit song yet from any of them? Why, thank you for asking. The answer is yes.

But none of it would have been possible without my Nashville angels Greg and Angie. They were there when I needed someone to give me a warm welcome, an encouraging word, a new fitness obsession, and a whole lot of connections. It's most definitely never too late to meet an angel or two. But it might also be time to be one to someone else.

twenty-seven
Write an Oratorio

I will be a ring of fire around her.
And I will be the glory in her midst.
And the power of my presence
Will bring her to her knees.
And I will lift her up again,
For I'm the God who sees.
I'm the God who sees.

—"THE GOD WHO SEES" BY KATHIE LEE
GIFFORD AND NICOLE C. MULLEN

Early in October 2018 I was in Nashville working on the music for *Then Came You*. I would normally stay at the fabulous apartment of my generous friend Wendy Hughes in the coolest section of downtown Nashville called the Gulch. It wasn't available this particular weekend, so Angie called her friend Beth Ingram to ask if I could stay in a lovely home she owned in the charming town of Franklin, about thirty minutes south of Nashville. Beth and her husband, Preston, are a philanthropic couple who do a tremendous amount of good in the area. They immediately agreed to let me stay.

Angie had set up a write for me with artist and songwriter Nicole C. Mullen. I had heard of Nicole's work and knew that she was a GRAMMY-nominated artist who had won multiple Dove Awards and was highly respected in the music and gospel worlds, but I'd never met her.

For no apparent reason, just prior to our meeting, I'd been mindful of the biblical character of Hagar. Hagar was the Egyptian handmaiden of Sarah, Abraham's barren wife, who, after a bitter fight with Sarah, was abandoned with her son, Ishmael, in the wilderness of an area called Beersheba. It's one of the most disturbing accounts in the story of Abraham and Sarah but, like every story in the Bible, all too human.

The other odd thing that had captivated me was a verse from Zechariah. Although I had read the Bible since I was a young girl (eleven times through in total), I didn't remember this scripture when I stumbled on it: "I . . . will be a wall of fire around her, and I will be the glory in her midst" (2:5 NASB). The sheer poetic beauty of these words stunned me and lingered with me. They were especially on my mind and heart the day Nicole arrived for our write.

Nicole is a magnificent, stylish, stately beauty with a natural elegance and a perfect smile. I liked her immediately. After a quick hello we settled onto sofas. She had brought her guitar but had also repeatedly warned me that she didn't play it very well, just enough to write a melody.

I laughed, "Well, I don't play at all. When I was a teenager my mother backed up over my guitar in our driveway and that was the end of that."

In the next hour I discovered that the Lord had recently placed Hagar on Nicole's heart as well. We agreed to write about her, incorporating the Zechariah scripture that He had revealed to me into the chorus. It was an easy, creative ebb and flow, and we ended our short session satisfied that we had the genesis of a solid song, which we hoped to pitch to Danny Gokey to record.

Nicole was preparing to leave the country to travel to Nigeria for ministry. I was leaving for home that afternoon, so we agreed that I would work on finishing the song while she was abroad.

A few days later, back in Connecticut, I sat down and began working on what we had written. I didn't stop with Hagar; I wrote about Ruth next, then David, and finally Mary Magdalene. Though it was not logical, I felt compelled to write it this way—a leading that I've learned to obey. Then I set it aside until Nicole and I could reconnect in Franklin and decide where to take it next.

We met a couple of weeks later at the studio of my producing partner, Sal Oliveri, to record a demo. By now it was obvious that we hadn't written a three-minute song; we had written a piece of theater, which needed a narration. Though I had written for theater for years, it was new for Nicole. She was honest with me when I asked her to go into the recording booth and, with no script, simply introduce each character before she started singing about them.

She looked at me with big, terrified eyes and said, "Oh, Kathie, I can't do that. I don't do that."

"No, Nicole," I told her. "It's not that you can't do that, it's just that you've never done it before. You know the Bible so well, just recount what you know about these characters and set the scene for us."

She shook her head, still not convinced of her abilities or the wisdom of doing this.

I chuckled, "Listen, this is just a demo. It's just you and me and Sal here, and anything you're not happy with we'll fix." (Do you recognize shades of Brett from a year earlier when we recorded "He Saw Jesus"?)

She finally agreed to try and walked into the recording booth, which is separated from Sal's engineering console by thick glass. Nicole stood in front of the microphone, Sal sat down at the keyboard directly across from her, and we began.

I had planned to take photos and record some video during the process, but that didn't happen because Nicole said these five simple words: "Hagar was a single mother." And boom! She didn't stop for the next eleven and a half minutes.

When she finished, Sal and I sat for a moment in hushed awe. Then I fell on my face thanking and worshiping God. Eventually I got up and walked over to where Sal was still sitting at the keyboard, his fingers trembling and tears streaming down his face.

"Not your typical demo day, is it, Sal?

He simply answered, "No."

I looked through the glass at Nicole, who was overwhelmed as well.

"Nicole," I said to her, "that was anointed of the Holy Spirit. There's no other way to explain what just happened."

She nodded and said, "I know."

After very few changes to what she had both said and sung, we knew we had the final version of *The God Who Sees*. It was not your typical song length at eleven and a half minutes long, but it was full of power and truth.

I was convinced Nicole's performance deserved to be showcased musically and decided right then to record it with musicians from the Nashville Symphony—one of the finest orchestras in the world. My recent book, *The Rock, the Road, and the Rabbi*, had been a surprise bestseller, and I knew in my heart I was supposed to take all the profits from it and underwrite the recording. The only logical step from there was to take our work to Israel and film this magnificent artist in the land where all the stories had actually happened. And so, we did.

For the first time in the more than fifty-five years of my crazy career, I put on a hat I'd never worn before: director. Then for four days, we filmed in the extraordinarily majestic, desolate, vibrant, resplendent promised land of my forefathers.

I felt reborn all over again. I was completely aware that every gift and every dream my Creator had placed in me in my mother's womb was finally being birthed. Everything I'd ever discovered and learned during every moment onstage, in front of cameras, microphones, audiences, and critics, was culminating in this experience. It was beyond humbling. It was beyond thrilling. Truly, if I had died the last time I hollered out, "Cut!" I would have died a soul-satisfied woman with no regrets.

But apparently God wasn't through with me yet. We headed home and I returned to *TODAY* for a few short weeks before April 5, 2019, the day I said a final goodbye to that wonderful, blessed season in my life. It was a bittersweet day wrapped in emotion and memories, but it was also filled with hope for the future and the "not yets" still ahead of me.

The God Who Sees was released that same day to unbelievable critical acclaim. But more importantly, it went into millions of homes and millions of hearts and changed thousands of lives. We know that from the comments we've received on YouTube.

How long has it been since you put on a new hat and stepped outside of your comfort zone? Maybe the story of Hagar can serve as a reminder to you that it's never too late. Because when two women who love Jesus sat down to write a song about another woman who thought nobody loved her, and when they followed in her footsteps by journeying out into the literal and metaphorical wilderness, incredible miracles took place.

twenty-eight
Get Weirdo

I'm ready to sing,
I'm ready to soar,
I'm ready to find what I was born for,
I'm ready to face the man I want to be,
Embrace my very own destiny.
Finally, I'm ready to love.
Finally,
Finally.

—"FINALLY" BY KATHIE LEE GIFFORD AND
CHUCK HARMONY & CLAUDE KELLY OF LOUIS
YORK FROM *THE GOD OF THE OTHER SIDE*

Nicole and I had just finished the demo of *The God Who Sees* when Angie asked me to come to her house and meet two of her newest friends, whom she called the weirdos.

"Why would I want to meet more weirdos?" I jokingly asked her. "I've been in show business my whole life."

She laughed her Angie laugh but then explained, "Because you're going to fall in love with them."

And she was right. From the moment she introduced me to Claude Kelly and Chuck Harmony, I was a goner. Separately they are responsible for bringing us some of pop music's biggest hits with artists like Michael Jackson, Whitney Houston, Beyoncé, Rihanna, Miley Cyrus, Bruno Mars, and Lady Gaga. You name the superstar and they've either written or produced that star's hits—or both.

Both were raised by single mothers who loved Jesus; Chuck in St. Louis and Claude in New York. Along with their industry successes they each were left with an aching emptiness in their souls and a deep longing for purpose in their lives and in their work. Independent of each other they left the music business—Claude to study the world's religions and Chuck to attend seminary.

They realized soon after that they shared the same disillusionment about the music industry and decided to move somewhere together to pursue a new "soul season." This time they worked with purpose, using their God-given gifts in a way that brought pride to their mothers and glory to the One who had borne their gifts in their mothers' wombs.

God led them to Franklin, Tennessee, just two doors down from, yes, Angie and Greg. Within days of moving in, Angie showed up on their doorstep with cookies, and the friendship began. She encouraged them to meet me and encouraged me to meet them, and all three of us asked the same question: Why?

"Because you need to, that's why."

She was right.

We all sat around Angie's kitchen table the first time we met and talked for hours. Although our details were different, our stories were the same—in spite of all the success in our lives, we each wanted more substance.

Angie made me play them the demo Nicole and I had just recorded with Sal. They sat and listened intently through the very last note.

"It's perfect," Claude said first.

"It is," Chuck agreed. "Don't change a single note."

Claude added, "Not a note."

Claude and Chuck had chosen the name Louis York as their stage name. Still, everyone called them the Weirdos because they had established a studio called the Weirdo Workshop where they dreamed, composed, recorded, and rehearsed their music. I started calling them "my boys" because that's what they had already become—treasured, trusted little brothers to me.

The following spring was my first write with the Weirdos. I greeted them at my first little townhome, poured them some GIFFT wine, and let them shuffle through a pile of my lyrics. They quickly agreed they wanted to write "Finally," an idea I had originally written for a future film, way down the road as one of the sequels to *Then Came You*. I initially envisioned it as a love song about a character who, after years of wasted living traveling the world as a musician, finally finds real love. We began writing with that intent.

When our lunch arrived we decided to take a break and eat. Angie suggested that while we ate we should watch *The God Who Sees*. It had just released, but Claude and Chuck had not yet seen it.

Not two minutes in they both shouted out various reactions of the same thing: "This is it! This is what we've been searching for! This is why we're here! This is how we're supposed to theatricalize our music!"

We were all excited, and I immediately blurted out, "Guys, this isn't supposed to be a love song about a man and a woman. This is supposed to be the ultimate love song between God and His children. The prodigal son! We're gonna write the next oratorio—*The God of the Other Side!*"

I said this with the utmost conviction because I knew it in my spirit. They did too. We all immediately said yes, then got back to work to finish the song, thrilled by our newfound purpose. In the end, we were totally satisfied with the first song we'd ever written together as a team. I was a Weirdo now, and it felt awesome.

A few weeks later we flew up to Connecticut for a long weekend to write the remaining songs of this larger project and record them in the studio at my home there. We had a blast and returned with the twenty-seven-and-a-half-minute demo.

I marvel at the way God works: He always does something abundantly better than anything we initially imagine. The song Nicole and I thought we were writing became *The God Who Sees*, and the song the boys and I were writing ultimately became *The God of the Other Side*. These writing journeys reminded me of the story in the Bible of the loaves and fishes: a small amount offered by a small boy turned into a miracle once given to Jesus, and it changed the world.

I remembered a conversation I'd had a few months before with my friend Donnadorable, who is a social contributor at *TODAY*. She had asked if she could listen to the symphony we had just recorded in Nashville.

"Of course," I'd told her and led her into my dressing room, placing my Bose headphones over her ears. Donnadorable is a twenty-eight-year-old gorgeous young woman born to secular Iranian parents. She's as hip and happening as they come, so I watched her intently as she listened. Near the end, tears were streaming down her beautiful face, and when it was over, she took the headphones off and said, "Oh my God, Kathie, this is a masterpiece!" (Her words, not mine, I swear.)

And then she said something that changed everything: "Can you make it longer? Can you add more stories? I've never heard these stories before!"

God used this precious young friend to show me the way forward. I was to keep telling the amazing stories that exist all through the Bible. I was to record them with the symphony. And I was to take the artists who performed them to Israel to bring the musical stories to life in film for a world that is "destroyed for lack of knowledge" of God's Word (Hos. 4:6 NASB).

I went over to hug Donna and tell her how grateful I was to her. She beamed.

Soon after I wrote two more oratorios: *The God of the How and When* with Brett James and Sal Oliveri for a film I was producing, and *The God of His Word* with my longtime friend and collaborator David Pomeranz (originally based on a series of songs we had written for Gladys Knight to perform in concert on the *TODAY* plaza).

Neither the film nor the concert ever came to fruition. They weren't supposed to. Because God had a different plan. A better plan than any of us had initially imagined.

Years ago God told me something I've never forgotten: "There are no crumbs on my table, Kathie. I use *everything* for good for My good purpose."

We Weirdos have just begun to work on our next oratorio, *The God of the Unknown*. Our desire is to tell the story of Jesus' birth as it really happened, not the Westernized, badly translated version the world has come to know and believe. Some may be angry with us for "messing with their manger." We're not trying to spoil Christmas for anyone; we're hoping to make it more alive and exciting and full of hope than ever.

It's never too late to get Weirdo! What might seem weird because we're not used to it ultimately becomes something beautiful that God created with the sole and "soul" purpose to delight us.

twenty-nine
Forgive

Lord, when I take stock of all the blessings I've been
   given,
The wondrous love that lives inside a heart that's
   been forgiven,
The blessed joy that lives inside a soul once lost in
   sin,
I lose my count as my blessings mount, so I begin
   again.
I can't begin to thank You, Lord.
There aren't enough hours in the day.
But I will try as each hour goes by
To send a smile Your way.

—"ABUNDANTLY" BY KATHIE LEE GIFFORD

Early in my career in New York, during the *Good Morning America* and *Live with Regis and Kathie Lee* days, I started hearing strange murmurs about Howard Stern, the number-one shock jock on the radio. I knew who he was, but I had never met him or listened to his program. I had heard that he mentioned me often—and with quite a bit of vitriol. It bewildered me. Why did he care about me? I certainly wasn't his enemy, but apparently early on he had decided to be mine. Maybe because we were both from the East Coast, the same age, and Jewish, yet polar opposites. I don't know why he chose to vilify me on a daily basis, but it went on incessantly for years.

I accepted it as an unfortunate part of reaching a certain level of fame. And honestly, I paid very little attention to it because I became busier than I'd ever been and finally happy after a long, lonely, and loveless marriage. I had married Frank Gifford, and God had blessed me with two precious children. Life was good. Regis and I were experiencing unprecedented success, redefining the landscape of daytime television, and reeling in the ratings.

I remember hearing or reading certain things that Howard had said and thinking, *He must be such an unhappy man. Bless him, Lord.*

In May 2012 Cody was graduating from the USC School of Cinematic Arts. I was going to fly to LA to attend the ceremony but first had to do my fourth-hour show. That morning I was in the hair and makeup chair getting ready when I happened to glance up at a monitor to see that Howard and his entourage were entering the studio one floor below to announce that he was joining the cast of NBC's *America's Got Talent*. It barely registered to me as important until I very clearly heard the Lord say, "Go downstairs and say hello to him. Wish him well."

I had long before learned to listen when God speaks to me, so I said internally, *Okay, Lord*, and got up to leave, shocking both Laura and Mary, my hair and makeup team.

"What are you doing? Where are you going?" they asked nervously.

"I'm going downstairs to say hello to Howard. I'll be right back."

They were totally stunned because apparently everyone in

the studio had been given strict instructions to make sure that Howard's and my paths never crossed. No one was expecting me when I entered Studio 1A and went directly over to Howard. I'm five feet, five inches tall and had wet hair, and I wasn't wearing any makeup. Because Howard is six feet six, he was completely oblivious to my presence beneath him.

"Howard? Howard?" I said looking directly up at him.

He looked around trying to find the voice. Finally, he looked down as I put my hand out to him and said, "Hi, Howard, I'm Kathie Lee. I think it's time we said hello, don't you?"

He was visually stunned and fumbled for a response. I didn't wait for one.

"I just want to wish you all the best on the new show."

I walked away and returned to the makeup room to finish getting ready. Laura and Mary were stunned, but I was totally at peace. Hoda and I did our show and then I flew to California as planned. When I landed and turned my phone back on to retrieve messages, there was a "No ID" voicemail. It was from Howard Stern. He basically said that he couldn't believe how kind I had been to him, that he was a jerk and he needed to talk to me.

I couldn't call him back because I didn't have his number. But a few hours later at dinner the same blocked call came up and I excused myself to answer the phone. Cody and Frank were not happy, but I knew I had to talk to him.

I stepped into a private room and the conversation went something like this:

"Kathie, I can't believe you were so nice to me. I'm so f–ed up, but I've been in therapy and I've been trying to get my sh*t together and say I'm so sorry. I've been a f–ing a-hole to you, and you don't deserve it, and I'm so sorry. And I need to ask you to forgive me." There were many more expletives, but you can use your imagination.

My heart felt so tender toward him I thought it would break. I said, "Howard, I'm so happy for you. The fact that you're asking for forgiveness from people that you've hurt is huge and so important. But you need to know that I forgave you years ago, and I've been praying for you every day since."

"You have?" he said.

"Yes," I said. "God loves you, and I know everything you said or did comes from a place of deep hurt and woundedness. It's okay, Howard. I'll keep praying that God continues to heal you." Then I asked him to come to dinner. An offer that caused Frank to have a fit! The dinner never happened, but I remember going back to my family and saying, "Okay, pigs are now officially flying all over the place."

It only took thirty years, but the day I left *TODAY* I came home to the biggest bouquet of flowers I have ever received—from Howard and Beth Stern, wishing me a wonderful new chapter in my life.

Unkindnesses come in all shapes and sizes, from those we love and even people we've never met. But life is too short to carry a grudge. Don't waste your time or your energy. Instead, drop the weight and forgive. The benefit often goes way beyond yourself. Don't let it be too late.

thirty

Play a New Game

I was a man who had everything,
Winter through summer through autumn through
> *spring,*
The pavement beneath and the stars up above,
'Til I came face-to-face-to-face
With something new, something called love.
I didn't know that I wasn't rich,
Had all I needed in my own little niche,
Nothing was missing that I could think of,
'Til I came face-to-face-to-face with something new,
> *something called love.*

—"SOMETHING CALLED LOVE" BY KATHIE LEE
GIFFORD FROM *UNDER THE BRIDGE*

This is a sentence I never dreamed I'd write: one beautiful summer day, Al Pacino came to my garden to have lunch with me.

I just had to reread that because I still can't believe it's a true story. (The best ones always are.)

I had met Al years before through our mutual longtime friend Anna Strasberg, who is the widow of the legendary acting coach Lee Strasberg. Lee developed methods for the Actors Studio, where famed actors like Marilyn Monroe, Paul Newman, and, yes, Al Pacino, studied. Al had seen my off-Broadway musical *Under the Bridge* and had instructed his assistant to call me about it.

"Hello, Mrs. Gifford. Mr. Pacino would like you to send him *The People Under the Stairs.*"

I laughed. "You mean *The Family Under the Bridge*?"

He laughed too. "Yes, please."

"Okay," I responded. "Does he want the screenplay or the stage version?"

"Both," he said, hedging his bets.

I sent them both and didn't hear a word for over a month. Hey, I was just thrilled Al Pacino loved my show!

Then one day his assistant called again. "Uh, Mr. Pacino would like to set up a meeting to discuss your project. He's presently in Los Angeles."

"Great!" I said. "I'm going to LA in a couple of weeks and I'd be delighted to meet with him."

On a beautiful January California day at the Beverly Hills Hotel, while I waited in the Polo Lounge restaurant with my friends Christine and Anna Strasberg, in walked Al Pacino in full movie star regalia—dark sunglasses and a long "Tony Curtis" scarf. He had just won the Golden Globe for Best Actor in the television miniseries *Angels in America*. All eyes followed him as he walked into the hotel courtyard and joined—gasp! What? Who?—Kathie Lee Gifford? It was great fun watching people freak out at the surreal coupling.

Al settled in and began to discuss the material, which he still couldn't believe I had written. "You know I've done some pretty good work in my life," he casually mentioned.

No kidding, I thought.

"But nothing my children can see." (His twins were very young at the time.) "And I love this script."

He then went on for about half an hour, digging into technical actor stuff about the character arc for Armand (the lead), the dynamic with the children, the antagonist . . . you get the picture.

I finally had to politely interrupt him because he had never mentioned the music, which I had cowritten with my friend David Pomeranz.

"Al, I'm sorry, but you *do* know this is a musical, right?"

He immediately looked at Anna and declared, "Why doesn't anyone think I can sing? I started my career in musical theater!"

Al was getting a little too much attention now from the already fascinated diners nearby, so I leaned over and quietly said to him, "I'm sorry, but you're just going to have to audition."

I thought he'd just chuckle at that, but no, Al immediately stood up, pushed himself away from the table, and began to sing "The Star-Spangled Banner," in full throat and totally in tune.

Everyone was stunned. Finally, I leaned over to him and said, "All right! You've got the job!"

It's one of my favorite moments to remember. After that, every time I'd see Al he'd say, "When are we going to make my movie?" God knows I'd been trying everything in my arsenal to get it made, but the timing was always off. Such is Hollywood. Some things happen overnight, others take more to come to fruition, and most never get done at all.

Which brings me to that fateful summer day at my house in Connecticut.

Al settled into a chair in my garden, and we began to chat like comfortable friends.

"You know, Al," I said, "I think I have one last book in me."

165

"Really?" he replied. "What's the name of it?"

"If You've Lived a Weirder Life Than Me, Then I Want to Meet You Before I Die."

Instantly he said, "Let's play!"

We began an epic game where I'd tell a true story, then he'd counter with a true story, and back and forth we'd go. He told me a story about Marilyn Monroe; I followed with one about the Kennedys. He parried with a fascinating Sir Laurence Olivier, and I answered with an Elizabeth Taylor, which he countered with an even better Elizabeth Taylor. It went on—deliciously—for two hours. We both were enjoying our back-and-forth thoroughly.

Finally, exhausted, I offered up my pièce de résistance. "Charles Manson," I said simply, for dramatic effect.

"What?" he shouted. "No way."

"Way," I responded, and I proceeded to tell him the following (again) true story.

Years ago I got a request from a wonderful friend of mine, Pastor Ray, to join him on a TV special he was going to tape at the California Men's Colony in San Luis Obispo, California. This was a maximum-security prison at the time and held a few thousand inmates.

"Pat Boone's going to be there too," Pastor Ray said. "Can you and Michie come as well?"

My sister, Michie, and I had joined Pastor Ray in his prison ministry several times before, and we had always been honored to be a part of his beautiful and Christlike outpouring of love to these broken men behind bars. So, naturally, I said we'd love to be a part of his television special.

A few weeks later Michie arrived ahead of me in San Luis Obispo.

"Okay, there's good news and bad news," she told me over the phone. "The good news is I just survived the worst turbulence in my life but landed safely here."

"Okay, good," I said. "What's the bad news?"

"The bad news is I just arrived at the prison and Tex Watson is my bodyguard."

"What!" I screamed. "Tex Watson, the man who actually butchered all the victims in the Manson murders?"

"Yes," Michie responded. "But, Kath, he's asked Jesus into his life, and I swear, he's a changed, redeemed man. His eyes are clear and beautiful and full of light. You're going to love him."

Love him? It was incredulous. Yet when I arrived I discovered that everything she had told me was true. Charles "Tex" Watson was a transformed creation in Christ, completely delivered from the drugs and the demons and the unspeakable violence of his former life under Charles Manson's influence. One look into his eyes convinced me of that.

It was 114 degrees outside when Michie and I arrived at the prison. We had been instructed to wear clothing that completely covered our bodies, from our necks to our wrists to our ankles, with no revealing flesh. No makeup, no jewelry. Nothing that could be considered at all alluring. In other words: Amish-like. The heat was already oppressive as we passed through the metal security checkpoints and heard the chilling sound of the electrified gates closing behind us.

Before long, we were assembled on the stage in front of thousands of California inmates—rapists, murderers, child molesters, you name it, they'd done it.

Pat Boone sang, Michie and I sang, Pastor Ray preached, and Tex shared his life-transforming testimony. The warden and his wife sat in the front row, and all was going well until suddenly the power went out and we were left stranded and vulnerable, struggling to adjust to the darkness in the already stifling amphitheater.

The terrifying reality of our situation quickly became apparent as prison guards rushed to remove the warden and his wife to safety, leaving Pastor Ray, Pat Boone, Tex Watson, and my sister and me alone on a dim stage. We held hands and sang "What a Friend We Have in Jesus" while thousands of hard-core inmates, many bare chested in the heat, yelled out "Sing 'Helter Skelter,'" and masturbated.

My life passed before me in the ensuing moments. I am ashamed to admit that I actually thought to myself, *I don't want to die looking like this.*

Suddenly the power came on and the guards were able to move all of us from the stage to safety.

When I finished the story, Al Pacino sat in stunned silence until he suddenly came to his feet, opened his arms wide, and cried out, "You win!"

thirty-one
Move Away from Home

I need to find my way home,
Back to where memories are deep as the dew,
Faded with time but still timeless and true,
Back to where soft breezes whisper a prayer,
In my heart, I'm already there.
In my heart, I'm already there.

—"MY WAY HOME" BY KATHIE LEE GIFFORD

Our 1920s Mediterranean home on Long Island Sound has been my favorite place in the world ever since we bought it and moved in on Cassidy's first birthday, August 2, 1994. Frank and I knew it was a miracle that we were able to purchase it. The house already had one offer on it from a wealthy Wall Street guy for way more than we could afford. But we made the best offer we could and started praying—barely breathing for four days while our realtor tried to seal the deal.

Finally, he called with the incredible news that the owner had agreed to sell the house to us.

"What? How did we get it? That's impossible!" we responded incredulously. "We offered way less."

The realtor told us, "I know. I'm telling you, in all my years in real estate I've never seen or heard anything like this."

It seems that years ago the owner had attended a pro-am tennis event for charity. He paid a lot of money to play tennis with an elite group of athletes. But when he arrived and went to sign in, he discovered that his name was nowhere on the list of attendees. He was upset and embarrassed until suddenly someone came up next to him, put his hand out to shake, and said, "Hi, I'm Frank Gifford. How would you like to play with me today?"

The realtor chuckled. "He was a huge Giants fan and now he was face-to-face with his favorite player of all time." All these years later, when it was time to decide whose offer to accept, he said, "I want Frank Gifford to own my house."

There was never a moment in all the ensuing years that Frank and I didn't marvel at the miracle. We kept expecting the real owners to show up at any moment and kick us out.

As the years passed, life brought many changes. Our kids moved to Southern California to pursue their dreams. Frank passed away in our sunroom and my precious mother, Joanie, died two years later. This once magnificent, bustling, filled-to-the-rafters-with-music-and-laughter home became a large, looming reminder of all that I had lost in my life. We'd had a daily tradition of toasting the sunset every evening. Now I'd go outside with my dogs and watch the dimming rays with crushing sadness.

I couldn't do it anymore.

I went through the motions for the next few years—getting up early, climbing in the car for the commute to New York, and smiling and laughing for our wonderful viewers one *TODAY* after another. No one but my family and my closest friends knew the depth of the depression I was battling. I cried out to God for an answer, and as always, He spoke to my heart from His Word. "I know the plans I have for you . . . plans to prosper you and not to harm you, plans to give you hope and a future" (Jer. 29:11).

Two years prior in 2017 I had given notice to my bosses at NBC that I would be leaving the show to finally follow my childhood dreams of movies and music. While they understood, they pleaded with me to stay and help them navigate the turbulent circumstances we were going through with the various personnel upheavals (Matt Lauer, Billy Bush, Megyn Kelly, to name a few) being played out on a daily basis in the media. It's not easy to report the news when you're actually making the news you're supposed to report.

I continued to stay until I just couldn't stay any longer. I've always had a keen sense of finality about certain things. I've come to understand it's a moving of the Holy Spirit—a voice I've learned to listen to and trust.

On April 5, 2019, after eleven amazing years with my now dear friend Hoda, I said goodbye to *TODAY* and hello to tomorrow. And with great joy, I got on a plane with Jill Martin, our fabulous fashionista on the show, and Joanne Lamarca, our executive producer, and flew to Nashville to celebrate.

I had purchased a small townhouse several months before, deciding it was best not to invest too much if it turned out that I wasn't as happy there as I had hoped. But I discovered almost immediately that Nashville was even more fun and exciting than I could have dreamed. I had a beautiful group of friends, a loving community of fellow believers, and an extraordinary pool of insanely talented writers to work with. The only thing I lacked was a home big enough to fit them all in. So, almost immediately I started looking for something larger.

I got into the habit of coming home after recording sessions and settling into my sofa on my small terrace to listen to the music I'd just been working on. It was cozy and comfortable. I'd often glance up, though, across a small alley next to me and see an exquisite townhouse three times as large as mine. I lusted after it. But the couple who lived there had designed and built the home themselves twelve years before and, by all accounts, had no plans to move. I kept looking.

One day while on my terrace, I heard a voice say, "Howdy, neighbor."

Carol introduced herself, waving from the aforementioned terrace I coveted.

"Oh, I'm so sorry," I said. "Am I playing the music too loud?"

"No," she said with a laugh. "I love it! Crank it up!"

I adored her immediately. We talked for about twenty minutes, then I blurted out, "If you and your husband ever decide to sell your beautiful home, would you consider calling me before you put it on the market? I'd be very interested in talking to you about it."

Carol smiled. I'm sure she heard that from somebody every day.

"Of course," she said and disappeared inside.

Five months later I was literally about to sign a contract on a house I'd found when the realtor who was showing it to me said, "You know, there's one more thing I want you to see before you buy this one."

"What is it?" I asked.

"It's one of the townhouses," he said.

"No, I've seen all of the ones that are available."

"Well, this one isn't even on the market yet, but the owners want to meet with you . . . it's the double-wide."

"What!" I shouted. "The double-wide? The one I lust after every day?"

"Yes."

The next morning I took my first step into Carol and Mike's townhouse. I knew instantly—I was home. I sat with them in their lovely living room and Carol teared up.

"You don't understand," she began. "Mike and I built this home twelve years ago. It took two years and we've loved every minute of it. We had no intention of moving anywhere. But two days ago I felt the Lord saying to me, 'I want you to sell your house to Kathie Lee to be the blessing to her that she's been to so many for so long.'"

I'm embarrassed to write this, but it's a huge part of the miracle, so I can't leave it out. Carol shared how she had been going through some difficult challenges in the years before. She would watch me on TV every day from her treadmill and feel inspired to keep going, keep believing, keep trusting that "God has this."

Now it was my turn to tear up.

"But where will you go?" I asked them.

"We have no idea," Carol laughed. "Do we, honey?"

"Nope," Mike said, laughing too.

"God will take care of us."

And He has. They are about to move into a brand-new home they built just a few blocks away from me. And I have no doubt we will be great friends for the rest of our lives.

thirty-two
Discover the World's Greatest Soul Singer

Yes, I gotta keep goin',
Gotta keep trustin',
Gotta stay strong.
And, Lord, I gotta keep singin'
My song my whole life long
Just the way You planned,
'Til I reach the promised land.

—"I GOTTA KEEP GOIN'" BY KATHIE LEE GIFFORD

Early in February 2019 Angie once again used her gift of connection to help me. She invited her friend Tom Morales to meet with me to learn about my wine and help me spread the word about it. A well-known and well-loved Nashvillian, Tom is generally credited with making Nashville the tourist mecca it has become. He owns several super-successful restaurants in town and the largest, yummiest catering company, TomKats, used on movie and television sets all over the world.

Tom is a bigger-than-life character. I was happy he had agreed to taste my wine and hopeful he would be willing to host some meet and greets at one of his famed restaurants.

We became instant friends because, well, everyone becomes instant friends with Tom.

One day, seven months later, Tom invited me to come to his big, bustling restaurant downtown called Acme Feed & Seed to hear a singer named Charles "Wigg" Walker. I had never heard of Wigg, but Tom assured me he was legendary in the Nashville music industry. Jimi Hendrix had been his guitarist. James Brown had kicked him off his tour bus because Wigg was pulling even better audience response than Brown.

"Nashville didn't become famous at first for country music, Kathie. It was black music first."

Cody and his fiancée, Erika, and Cass and her fiancé, Ben, happened to be visiting that weekend. They joined me, Angie, and Greg and we headed downtown.

Wigg was already singing when we arrived. I simply could not believe the sound that was coming from this thin, frail, seventy-nine-year-old man. It was the purest, most thrilling voice you can imagine. Powerful beyond description. And seemingly effortless. I was mesmerized. I couldn't sit still. I had to get up and groove to the music he was making. Wigg noticed and very sweetly said hello from the stage.

Suddenly Tom said, "Go up there and sing with him, Kathie."

"What? No way!" I told him.

But Tom insisted, and Tom is used to charming everyone to do what he wants. So, I went onstage.

I can't describe what singing with Wigg was like except that he made me fearless. Brett James had bamboozled me to sing again a couple years before, but Wigg made me sing notes I've never hit before. With no rehearsal, no warm-up, no finding the right key, I simply joined him on his journey. It was musical magic for me from the very first note.

Wigg was happy, too, and so it began that each time I came to hear him at Acme I'd join him onstage for a few songs.

Tom and I agreed that we needed to produce a documentary about Wigg and an album to go with it. That's what we're working on now. It's been so thrilling to share some of my songs with Wigg, which he immediately wanted to record. I can't wait for the world to hear him—his music and his story.

A weirder musical duo you could never imagine—far more surprising than Lady Gaga and Tony Bennett—but this is the crazy stuff of my life these days, and I believe there is joy and newness waiting just around the corner for you too.

thirty-three
Go on Your First Date in Thirty-Three Years

Just when I thought the sun could no longer warm me,
Just when I felt spring had no more allure,
Just when I was sure that I'd heard every lovely melody,
Every lovely song,
You came along.
I was wrong.

—"I WAS WRONG" BY KATHIE LEE GIFFORD

I had been in Nashville a few months when Angie and Greg invited me to go to a club to hear one of the best bands in town: Tim Akers & the Smoking Section. I was grooving to the fabulous music when an attractive man who had smiled at me earlier tapped me on the shoulder and asked me to dance.

We danced, and he promptly disappeared into the packed house.

Well, that was fun, I thought and went back to enjoying the show.

Two weeks later, at a music festival with my same friends and the same band, the mysterious man reappeared.

"So, you came back for more, huh?" I teased him, and this time we danced a lot longer. Then, you guessed it, he simply disappeared into the packed crowd.

I guess I'm a lousy dancer, I laughed to myself. But just as I was leaving for home, he came up to me and thanked me for dancing with him the second time.

"Well, what are you going to do about it?" I asked him.

"What?" he replied, a little stunned.

So, I asked him again, "What are you going to do about it?"

He stammered a bit but finally admitted, "Well, I'm a little intimidated by you."

"Why?" I asked.

"Because you're Kathie Lee Gifford."

"No, I'm not. I'm just a woman," I said. Though what I really wanted to say was, "No, I'm not. I'm Kelly Ripa." That always gets a laugh.

"You mean it's okay to get your number and give you a call?" he said.

"Yes," I answered. "You seem like a very nice guy."

I gave him my number, to which he commented, "Well, now you have my number too."

"Oh no," I said, shaking my head. "I will never call you. I'm old-fashioned that way."

Then I looked at him and said, "And if you *don't* call me, I will never dance with you again." Finally, it was my turn to disappear into the night.

I'm not sure if I left him traumatized or energized, but he did call, and we spent a fun couple of weeks dancing all over town.

He was nice. He was sweet to me, yet I knew from the beginning it wasn't going to turn into anything other than that. We lived very different lives, and mine was about to get busy and hectic again with movies, oratorios, and Israel. He understood, and I know we both said goodbye with a sense of gratitude for our fun time together.

I learned that I could enjoy a man's company and affection again after Frank's passing. And who knows? Next time it might turn out differently.

Actually, two years earlier, which was two years after Frank died, I was sitting outside in front of a fire next to the sunroom—the room where Frank had breathed his last. I was enjoying a beautiful summer evening with a good friend. We'd been talking about our lives and our journeys, our heartbreaks and our heartstrings—deep stuff—as only trusted friends can.

"So, I guess Frank was the love of your life," he declared more than asked.

"So far," I answered. My answer surprised even me.

He sighed. "I've never had a love like that."

I recognized the longing and said, "You will someday. God has great things in store for those who love Him."

He wasn't sure.

I think a lot of people doubt that God actually longs for His children to be happy, in love, healthy, and prosperous. In spite of all the trouble He warned us we'd have, the Scriptures are full of messages of hope.

So many people ask me if I think I'll ever get married again. "I have no idea," I always answer. "I don't know what my future holds, but I know the One who holds my future."

I don't mean it to sound like some pat cliché. I say it because I know it's true. I've been blessed with a great love, and only God knows if Frank was my last one. Honestly, I hope not. I have such a full, vibrant, and exciting life. I'd love nothing more than to share it with someone who understands it, values it, and enjoys it as much as I do.

That's an intimidating thing to many men. They're not used to strong, independent women who know what they want and refuse to settle for less than what God desires for them. Men have tried to control history for so long that they're resistant to sharing the reins. But I'm okay with that. Any man who's afraid *of* me is not the man *for* me.

I love Proverbs 31, which says of the godly woman: "She laughs at the future" (v. 25 LEB).

That's where I find myself now—feeling decades younger than I obviously am. "Fired up," as my friend George Shinn calls it, with God's endless promises and possibilities.

Psalm 5:3 says, "In the morning, LORD, you hear my voice; in the morning I lay my requests before you and wait expectantly." I smile when I read that every morning. I actually transpose it just a bit to read "wait in *expect* and *see!*"

I believe in an all-loving, all-seeing, all-good, gift-giving God. My oratorios are all about His character—His shalom: faithfulness, loving-kindness, justice, benevolence, joyfulness, peacefulness, and righteousness. He sees me. He sees you. And the greatest miracle? He loves us anyway.

The greatest way to make the most outrageous, transformational change in your life at *any time* of your life is right here, right now. *Believe Him.*

It's not too late.

thirty-four
Keep Up with the Kardashians

I've lived enough and survived enough to freely speak
   my mind.
And it's liberating anticipating the reactions that I
   find:
My mother is aghast, my husband is bemused,
My friends in far-right places, well,
They're not all amused.
My children think I'm crazy, and I tell them that's
   just fine
'Cause if I have to lose something,
I'd prefer to lose my mind.

—"ESTROGEN BLUES" BY KATHIE LEE
GIFFORD FROM THE MUSICAL *HATS*

Kris Jenner and I have been friends since the late 1970s when I moved to LA to pursue my career. To say we have been through thick and thin together doesn't come close to expressing the depth of it. I met her when she was married to her first husband, Robert

Kardashian, and had very young children. We studied the Bible together, and then, as is often the case, lost touch in 1982 when I moved to New York to do *Good Morning America*.

We reconnected when Frank and I were at Ethel Kennedy's home in Hyannis Port, Massachusetts, for a Robert F. Kennedy celebrity tennis tournament. Bruce Jenner was a guest as well. Frank and I had both befriended him as colleagues through *Good Morning America*. He was elated when we ran into him at Ethel's. I asked him what was going on.

"I've met the most amazing woman," he gushed.

"I'm so happy for you," I said. "Do I know her?"

"No, she isn't in the business, thank God," he answered. "Her name is Kris Kardashian."

"I love her!" I shouted. "We used to be great friends. We've just lost touch."

The rest, of course, is a story that the world knows all too well. Bruce and Kris got married and had two more children—daughters Kendall and Kylie. Frank and I were asked to be their godparents, and we joyfully agreed.

What very few people know is that at that time, the family was in difficult financial straits. Kris was managing Bruce's career, but he was no longer the super sports hero du jour and wasn't pulling in the lucrative endorsement or appearance money he once had. As they say, fame is fleeting. I kept praying with Kris as they struggled, moving from one rental home to another in order to survive.

I sent my two goddaughters a darling Amish-made playhouse. It was just like the one I had purchased for Cassidy at our house. I included all the precious furniture and accessories for it, hoping it would bring the girls the same pleasure it had brought to Cass. They loved it.

Then one day I was talking to my new agent at the William

Morris Agency. She once again wanted me to consider doing a reality series—something I had resisted for years.

"No," I told her for the umpteenth time. "But you should do one with Kris and Bruce Jenner. That would be just unbelievable."

It was true. Life in the Jenner home was a perpetual funny, crazy roller coaster of a ride. A circus. In one door, the Giffords, and out another door, the Jackson family, Wayne Gretzky, Scott Hamilton, O. J. Simpson—you name them. They were all a part of the Jenners' everyday lives.

"No!" she answered me, very strongly. "I wouldn't touch them with a ten-foot pole. But I do represent Ryan Seacrest, and I think he'd be interested."

Soon after, the world as we knew it came to an end.

Keeping Up with the Kardashians premiered in October 2007 and began a worldwide, frenzied phenomenon that continues to this day. I remember when the first episode premiered. I was nervous because I knew all too well how producers will manipulate anything they can to heighten the tension, increase the drama, and ensure they get a hit.

"Kris," I warned my friend, "I know you're excited about this, but please make sure you insist on some creative control. Make sure they represent you accurately. Make sure they show you saying grace over the food and going to church. It's important."

"Oh, I will," she assured me. "I'm one of the executive producers."

"Good," I told her. "You go, girlfriend."

Cassidy and her godmother, Christine (aka Chrissie, my right and left hand), and I waited at her house for the premiere. We had intentionally gone there to avoid Frank watching it with us at home. I somehow knew he would hate it. The show began and the three of us sat there speechless with the rest of the world. Finally, when it was over, I asked Cassidy, who was fourteen at the time, "What did you think, honey?"

"But, Mom," she answered, confused, "they're not like that."

Kris waited to hear from me. She wanted to know what I had thought. But I hesitated to call her, as I always do when I'm not sure how to say what I know I need to say. This was a family I dearly loved. This was a friend I prayed with about *everything*. Now her family was on the verge of the kind of fame that was truly going to change *everything*. I was happy for her and terrified for her at the same time. Finally, I called.

Everyone knows what happened after that. But through it all, my friendship with Kris and my love for her family remained steadfast. If you are my friend, you are my friend forever. People ask me all the time if I had any knowledge of Bruce Jenner's decision about his gender during that time. No, I didn't. Bruce and Frank were very close. There were very few men that Frank considered his peers, but Bruce was one of them. Frank wasn't arrogant about his fame and his accomplishments, but very few men had ever achieved his level of success in one of the most difficult arenas in the world—sports.

Frank admired Bruce enormously. He had covered the 1976 Olympic Games in Montreal where Bruce stunned the world when he won the gold medal in the decathlon, basically crowning him the greatest athlete in the world. And Frank liked Bruce as a person. Bruce was affable and fun. He was also dyslexic. Frank could relate because, as a young man, he had stuttered. So, Frank mentored Bruce in the television world, just as he mentored me. He taught him about the ins and outs of professional sportscasting, and he took great pride as he watched Bruce navigate the treacherous new waters of being in front of the camera.

Frank was as stunned and taken by surprise as the rest of the world when Bruce identified as a woman and announced that he wanted to change his gender.

"Well, I'll be," is all I remember him saying. "I never saw that coming."

By that time Bruce and Kris had divorced and were living separate lives. Several days before the infamous interview with Diane Sawyer was scheduled to air, Bruce called me. I was happy to hear his familiar, distinctive voice.

"Kathie," he said after we exchanged pleasantries, "do you hate me?"

"Hate you?" I exclaimed, "Of course not, Bruce. I could never hate you. I love you."

"But your faith . . ." he started.

I prayed silently that God would give me the grace to speak words of hope and life to my sweet friend.

"Bruce, God created you. You may believe He made a mistake with you, but God doesn't make mistakes. We do."

He was silent on the other end of the line.

"Sweetie, He knows you. He sees you. He loves you."

My heart beat heavily in my chest.

"Whatever you do to your body—whatever changes you make—you can never change the masterpiece you are that He created. He created you in His image. And when you die, as we all will, that body will decay. Ashes to ashes, dust to dust. But the eternal part of you—your soul—will go on forever. And He will make you perfect. That is the hope of eternal life in Him."

I could sense him taking this in, processing the enormity and wonder and miracle of it.

"Thank you, Kath," he simply said.

"Are you going to change your name?" I asked. By now my heart was broken because his was.

"Yes," he said, "to Caitlyn."

"It's a beautiful name," I said. And it is. "I love you, Caitlyn."

She called me just once again, soon after. And we tried to get together in New York City, but our schedules were crazy because life is crazy. It changes every nanosecond. But God doesn't. He is the same yesterday, today, and forever. He loves us. His heart breaks for us. But He never gives up on us. It's never too late to tell your friends that God loves them.

I recently attended Kanye West's Sunday Service in Burbank. I had first heard of the now world-renowned rapper years before when he had one of his first hits, a song called "Jesus Walks." People kept asking me if I'd heard that I'd been mentioned in this great new song by Kanye West. The lyrics went: "The way Kathie Lee needed Regis, that's the way I need Jesus."

I still haven't heard the song. But the whole world has now heard of Kanye.

I was looking forward to personally experiencing what many friends I respected had assured me was a truly genuine faith-filled expression of God's redeeming love. My longtime friend Lesley Burbridge had just taken the position of press agent for Kanye, so she picked me up early Sunday morning at my hotel to take me to the service. I had called Kris Jenner the day before in the hopes that she would be attending and was thrilled when she told me, "I will be now!"

After Kanye's extraordinary service, I got in the car with his wife, Kim Kardashian, and her absolutely gorgeous children to travel north on the Ventura Freeway to join the whole Kardashian family at Kylie's house in Hidden Hills.

Kylie Jenner was by now the world's youngest self-made billionaire, featured on the cover of *Forbes* magazine. And she was having a launch party for her new line of children's products named after her daughter, Stormi.

I hadn't seen Kim in a long time. She seemed extra tiny next to me, holding her newest child, Psalm. The radio was on low, but the driver turned up the volume when he heard a reporter give an update about potential traffic problems ahead due to a helicopter accident in the area. I remember silently praying for whomever was on that helicopter while Kim continued to tell us about all she was doing to become a lawyer so she could free people from incarceration in our antiquated prison system. My heart swelled with pride for her.

"You're doing the work Jesus called us to do, Kim," I told her. "Set the prisoners free."

This gorgeous woman, now a mother of four, nodded her head. "I know," she said.

"And everything you've been through has brought you to this moment. No one would care if you weren't Kim Kardashian. Every one of the people you've worked to release, and every one of their stories, would be ignored if it weren't for all that you've been through." Then I quoted from Romans 8:28: "All things work together for good to those who love God and are called according to His purpose" (RGT).

Her beautiful, soulful eyes filled with tears.

"I know," she said as we pulled up in front of Kylie's house.

I hadn't seen Kylie since the premiere of Cassidy's 2015 movie, *The Gallows.* And I hadn't met Stormi yet, so I was excited to hug them both and reconnect when the news hit: Kobe Bryant and his thirteen-year-old daughter had perished in that helicopter crash we had just heard about on the radio.

Instantly the atmosphere changed. Everyone huddled with their phones for more news. Kobe and Vanessa and their four beautiful children were good friends of the Kardashian/Jenner family. They'd recently spent New Year's Eve together.

Everyone tried, in their own way, to make sense of the senseless.

We prayed for Vanessa and her now three children. We prayed for the other families who lost loved ones as the details of the crash began to emerge. I had no idea how many hours had passed when Kris got up and suddenly said, "Come here, Kathie. I want to show you something in the backyard."

I dutifully followed her into Kylie's immaculate, fairy-filled backyard. Kris led me to a delightful little house nestled among the trees.

"Remember, Kath?" she said with a smile. "This is the playhouse you had made for Kendall and Kylie when they were little girls. I had it refurbished when Stormi was born."

I was stunned. It was beyond beautiful.

"But look," she continued, opening the little door, "I kept all the original furniture and the little stove and the little refrigerator and all the dishes, pots, and pans."

I could hear our Savior speaking to me, drawing on the wisdom in Isaiah 43:19: "Behold, I make all things new, Kathie! Do you not perceive it?"

A few moments later Kylie found me. She was holding a tiny charm bracelet.

"You gave me this, right?" she asked as I focused on the little Tiffany treasure. "I'm saving it now for Stormi."

To which Kendall—all five-feet-ten-perfect-model inches of her—responded, "And I look at the picture of you and me every morning next to my sink in my bathroom."

As I sat in the car on my way back to my hotel, I marveled once again at the faithfulness of God and His unfailing love. I have been criticized for years for my continued association with this family, but I couldn't care less what people think. The Word of God says that the world will know we are Christians by our love for one another (John 13:35).

I received so much criticism from Christians early in my career, basically asking me, "How can you call yourself a Christian and be in show business?"

To which I always replied, "How can I be in show business and *not* be a Christian?" There is simply no way I could have survived the constant rejection and brutality—both psychological and physical at times—that are part and parcel with show business. I knew God had called me to this business. He knew His plans for me in my mother's womb. He saw me being formed. And He saw all the millions of people who would eventually hear about Jesus because He placed a boldness in me to proclaim His truth to the masses.

There is no doubt in my mind or in my spirit that Kanye loves Jesus with all his heart. I know a lot of people think he started a cult, but I stood for ninety minutes at his Sunday service and there was not one word—either spoken or sung—that did not proclaim anything but the worship of Jesus, the Messiah. Every church should be such a cult!

And I can see God moving in the hearts of each and every member of the Kardashian/Jenner clan. No one has the right to judge another person. Besides, the same judgment we declare over others will be declared over we who do the judging (Matt. 7:1–2). We need to remind ourselves every day that "all have sinned and fall short of the glory of God" (Rom. 3:23).

All means all—you and I and everyone else on the planet. God desires that we love one another and leave the judging to the only One who ever lived a perfect life, which He willingly gave up that we might have life and life abundant (John 10:10).

After all, "We love Him because He loved us first" (1 John 4:19 RGT).

thirty-five
Applaud with the Audience
and Cheer On a Friend

Don't be afraid of the road you can't see
Or the strangers you don't know by name.
For in the blink of an eye, mysteriously,
Your life will never be the same.

—"YOU WILL MEET WITH ADVENTURE TODAY" BY
KATHIE LEE GIFFORD FROM *UNDER THE BRIDGE*

As my deadline for this book approached, my former agent and friend Sam Haskell called me and asked that I accept an award he had nominated me for: Movieguide's Visionary Award, which I would receive in LA on January 24, 2020. If anyone but Sam had asked me, I'd have said no because I simply didn't have time. But Sam is one of my special few, so I agreed.

Then I learned that Regis would be giving me the award, and I was thrilled. I hadn't seen him and Joy since the July before when I was home in Greenwich for a rare weekend with my Weirdos, working on *The God of the Other Side*.

To say it was a long evening is an understatement. The red carpet lasted more than an hour, the reception another hour, and then finally the audience assembled for the taping of what would end up becoming a Hallmark primetime special a month later.

But Regis hadn't arrived, and I became concerned. He was eighty-eight then, and I had noticed that he was slowing down in his physicality and ability to process the world around him. Joy, his wonderful wife of fifty years, was ever present, protecting him. I remembered all the times I had attempted to do that for Frank too. God bless the caretakers.

My award would be among the last of the evening that was now close to six hours in coming. And with just minutes before it was scheduled, Regis and Joy finally arrived.

"Oh, Lord," I prayed, "please be with him. Protect him and give him all the strength he needs for this moment."

Regis was taken backstage to make his entrance. I whispered yet another prayer for him and one for myself. "Lord, give me the words to say. Please, Lord, I have no idea why I'm here or what Your purpose is. Just speak through me."

I have *never* written a speech. I have always just asked God to lead me, and He always has. Always. So, I waited nervously for Reege to take the stage. Finally, he did, and to much love and applause from the audience. I was happy to hear the reaction of yet another audience that has enjoyed and appreciated him for so long. But then he began to struggle with the teleprompter. He got a little confused, and I could sense the audience's concern for him too. Finally, he said, "And in my forty-five years in this business I spent fifteen of them with Kathie Lee, and they were the best fifteen years in my whole career."

I smiled.

"So, let's bring her onstage right now to accept the Visionary Award—Kathie Lee . . . *Griffin!*"

The audience gasped.

I was thrilled and threw myself to my feet, seizing the golden opportunity.

"It's *Gifford*," I yelled at him. Regis looked for the voice.

"It is?" he asked, and the audience roared. "Are you sure?"

The audience went wild. It was the only unscripted, genuinely funny moment of the very long evening. As I approached the stage to accept the award, I thanked the Lord for bringing us back to the classic *Live with Regis and Kathie Lee* days. It was a gift.

A lovely young lady handed me the award, and with joy, I hugged this dear friend of mine. "You're killing me," I whispered in his ear, then turned to the audience and said, "And you think you know somebody!"

Oh, I know him, all right. And I cherish his friendship. I cherish the memories, and I cherish all the moments we shared when we had the privilege of making America laugh.

I have another friend who has weathered many public and private memories with me—Hoda Kotb. It's late March as I write this, and I watched her break down today on the show. She has been anchoring with Savannah Guthrie in isolation due to COVID-19.

Hoda was interviewing one of her favorite people from one of her favorite cities—Drew Brees from New Orleans—as he announced his extraordinary gift of $5 million to battle the pandemic in their beloved city.

"Something else is contagious too," Hoda told him, "generosity."

And then she simply began to give in to the raw emotion and frazzled nerves and sheer exhaustion of showing up for weeks trying to do her job with her usual grace, professionalism, and passion. I think it was the defining moment of her extraordinary career.

I wept with her. That's her gift. She shows up authentic and optimistic and then she smiles that Hoda smile and laughs that Hoda laugh, and sometimes—in rare, unpredictable moments—she cries those Hoda tears.

That's why I love her. That's why everybody loves her. I stayed at *TODAY* ten years longer than I had planned because I fell in love with her.

I've been gone more than a year now, and I miss sitting next to her every day. I have watched her evolve from an award-winning journalist, *Dateline* Hoda, into an extraordinarily natural and captivating television presence, Happy Hour Hoda.

She was just awarded yet another Emmy for her rock-solid coverage of this pandemic, but all she cares about is rushing home to her family—Joel and Haley and Hope—and creating another memory.

I celebrate her. I admire her. I love her to pieces. And I lift up my glass as we did countless times and say, "Brava, Hoda Mama! You're the best."

I've been incredibly blessed to have several truly best friends—Regis and Hoda are simply two prime examples. A real friend makes you feel better about yourself. Friends help you cope when you think you're done and offer hope that it can get better. They love you as you are but won't let you stay that way. Clearly, having friends improves our lives. And best friends? They make every good thing even better.

A Pulse and a Purpose

The year 2019 has come to an end. I've just spent the holidays with my kids and their betrotheds, and I'm excited to watch their happiness and their myriad hopes for the future come to fruition. There is nothing like love, and I know God will guide their futures just as He has guided mine all these faithful years.

We are all healing. We miss Frank every day, and there are constant reminders of him everywhere. But we all have dreams yet to fulfill and much work to do. We're grateful the laughter has returned.

I look forward to someday being a grandmother—or, better yet, "Glam-ma!" But that, too, is in God's hands and timing. I will release two new books in the coming year, three films featuring the oratorios shot in Israel, the third Hallmark film, and the movie *Then Came You*. And I will receive a star on the Hollywood Walk of Fame. (All dependent on what happens with the COVID-19 virus, of course.)

None of this overwhelms me; it excites and inspires me. Because if I wake up every morning and I still have a pulse, that means I still have a purpose too. Paul Newman taught me that years ago.

It was a bitterly cold Sunday night, and I had left Frank sitting by a blazing fire watching football. I had promised many weeks earlier to attend a fundraiser for the Westport Country Playhouse at a home two coves over from ours.

I remember driving there on the icy road and thinking, *Why did I say yes to this?*

Soon after I arrived I heard a commotion near the front door. I turned around to see who was causing it. Paul Newman, who always sent both women and men into a frenzy, had just walked in. I didn't want to be yet another pushy person vying for his attention, so I moved into the next room, hoping I'd get a chance to say hello later in the evening.

Paul had been my very first celebrity interview when I started on *Good Morning America*. Just as I was about to ask my first question, I completely lost my composure. I was speechless. I couldn't believe I was standing there with Paul Newman as if it were the most natural thing in the world. *It wasn't.*

I apologized profusely, but he just flashed that megawatt smile and looked at me with those amazing eyes and said something like, "Ah, don't worry about it. What do you want to ask me? You'll be fine."

He was so kind. Later, we became friends when I started working with his incredible charity for sick children at the Hole in the Wall Gang Camp. Both Frank and I adored him.

Several minutes after I had moved into the next room, I felt a tap on my back. I turned around and there was Paul. He immediately got down on one knee, took both of my hands in both of his, kissed them, and said, "Hi, Kathie. How are you?"

It was surreal. I said, "Oh, Paul, it's so good to see you! It's been too long. How are you?"

He struggled a little to get up and said, "Honey, I'm eighty years old but I've still got a pulse. And that's a good thing."

I remember going home and telling Frank the story and how moved I was that Paul Newman was still using his celebrity to make the world a better place—even a dilapidated old theater in Connecticut.

Frank didn't buy it. "You just love his eyes," he said with a laugh.

As I went to bed that night, I knew Paul had taught me something that I'd take with me for the rest of my life: if I have a pulse, I have a purpose. And you do too. It affected me enough that I wrote a song about it.

If I have a pulse

I have a chance

To change someone else's circumstance.

If I have a pulse

I have a privilege

To save someone who's on the edge.

CHORUS:

If my heart is still beating when I awake

I can change someone's world for heaven's sake.

If I have a pulse

I've an opportunity

To lead that soul into eternity.

If I have a pulse,

If I have a pulse.

There are so many more stories I wish I could tell you: some crazy, some heartwarming, some heartbreaking, and many just too incredible to be true. But I can't because the people involved matter to me, and they've asked me not to share them. They needn't worry. Their secrets are safe with me. And I pray to God that my secrets are safe with them. It's never too late to keep a secret and save a friend, right?

None of us knows when we will breathe our last breath. Frank didn't, my parents didn't, and I won't either. But I know where I'm going, and I know who is waiting for me there. I have great peace in my soul from walking with my Savior since I was twelve years old, discovering through every day of every decade that *God is faithful in all things and in all ways.*

I pray that on the day I die I will have learned something brand-new or will have done something I've never done before or written the best lyric He's ever given me.

Because it's never too late until, yes, one day it actually is.

Let's not waste a moment.

Bless you.

He Made Us Laugh

And then one day, when no one expected it, Regis died.

Those of us who knew him best and spent time with him in the last two years of his life could sadly see the inevitable coming. It was the same with Frank, and my mother and father. They began disappearing little by little. They changed in small ways, and then the changes began to accelerate. Finally, they began sleeping more, eating less, and losing interest in the things they once loved. It's heartbreaking when it happens, but it does help you prepare emotionally for your final goodbye.

In June 2020 I was home in Connecticut for a rare visit. As I always did, I invited Regis and Joy to come to my house for lunch. It was something Regis had loved to do since Frank and I moved into our house almost twenty-six years earlier. Regis always had so much fun roaming around, pointing to a table or a firepit surrounded by sofas and exclaiming, "And yet *another* place to *eat!*" Sometimes he'd even call me and ask if he could bring people over—people I didn't even know—and take them on a tour.

"Sure, Reege, but I'm not even home," I'd say.

"Who cares?" he'd laugh, and I'd laugh right along with him. Then he'd hang up and come right over. Lord, he made me laugh. He made *everyone* laugh.

Regis could walk into a United Nations gathering filled with people from all over the world who spoke thirty different languages and have them all in stitches within thirty seconds. He never had an enemy because he never made one. He was kind to everyone, took notice of everyone, and if he really liked someone, he would tease them mercilessly. Yes, that was the ultimate Regis Philbin "seal of approval" compliment.

I was entirely charmed by him for thirty-five years, along with the rest of the world. But there were many, many private times with him as well that were much more serious in nature. I cherish the memories of those as well.

Regis had been raised in the Catholic faith and, like many of my Catholic friends, had questions about the deep issues facing the church. He was brokenhearted when he learned of any scandals or lawsuits and hated seeing parochial schools closing at an alarming rate. He genuinely feared for not just the future of his religion but of our nation.

"What do you think is going to happen, Kath?" he'd often ask me. And I'd answer as carefully as I could from my studies of Scripture.

I know without a doubt that Regis believed that Jesus was the Son of God and that He died to save the world from sin. Regis had a simple, sweet faith, the kind that makes God smile.

So on that day in June, I watched from my front door as Regis and Joy, as they had a hundred times before, drove up my driveway and parked in our courtyard.

Regis got out on the passenger side of their car. I immediately saw that he was much more frail than he'd been some six months prior when I saw him in LA. We sat in my screened porch and enjoyed a delicious lunch of his favorite, frutti di mare, and laughed as we had for almost four decades.

At one point I said to him, "Reege, you still have a great head of hair!"

Joy couldn't help saying, "You hear that, Regis? Tell Kathie what you said this morning."

Regis looked at her and asked, "What did I say?"

Maybe he didn't remember, or maybe he was setting her up for a joke. I could never tell. But Joy didn't bite this time. She looked at me and said, "Regis got up this morning and said, 'We're going to see Kathie today, right?'"

"Yes, honey, we're going to her house for lunch."

Then Joy began to giggle as she looked at me and continued. "So Regis said, 'I don't like my hair today. Wash it and blow-dry it for me, Joy. I want to look good for Kathie.'"

I was so touched, and Regis just beamed. He knew he looked handsome!

After several hours they hugged me goodbye and got into their car to drive home.

I was happy/sad, you know? So happy to see my precious friend again, but so sad to admit that it might have been for the last time.

A few weeks later, back in Tennessee, I felt the Lord telling me to get on the next plane in the morning and go home. I had no idea why, but I have learned through the years not to ignore His promptings. I had no sooner walked into my door in Connecticut when my friend Angie texted me, "I'm so sorry about Regis ☹."

"What?" I texted back, and she told me the news that Regis had passed. I was stunned but not surprised. I actually rejoiced, just as I had when I had held Frank in my arms just moments after his passing, almost five years earlier.

And just like Frank, Regis was with Jesus. He was truly home.

The next day I drove over to see Joy and her beautiful daughters, Joanna and J. J., carrying a vat of frutti di mare and bottles of GIFFT wine. I found them in the living room going through boxes and boxes of pictures, each more precious than the last one.

"Beloved!" I said to them. "They're finally using the word *beloved* in every article—in every tribute to Regis—because that's what he is."

I didn't stay long. As Joy walked me to the door, she told me something I will never forget for the rest of my days.

"He hadn't laughed for a long time, Kathie, and I was truly getting worried about him. But then we came to your house for lunch, and you both just picked up right where you left off the time before."

I nodded, remembering, tearing up.

"That was the last time I heard Regis laugh."

One Final Thought

If I'm honest, and I truly do try to be, I have only been in love three times in my life. I've been married twice, dated many men, and made too many bad choices through the years, in both my personal and my professional lives.

I've walked the walk of shame. I've been sexually harassed, sexually abused, and date raped.

I have tried to live a life of integrity, and more times than I want to admit, I have failed miserably.

I've smiled many phony smiles when I was aching to cry real tears.

I've railed at God privately while publicly praising Him.

I have cared way too often what other people thought of me and thought way too much of myself way too many times.

I have tried to please people who don't matter instead of pleasing my Creator, the only One who does.

I have achieved great heights, and I have hit rock bottom.

I have been lied about, and I have lied too.

I have lived with great sorrow and profound poverty of my soul.

I have sinned.

But I have been forgiven.

I am a child of God.

I Want to Matter

by Kathie Lee Gifford

I want to matter,
To have meant something special to somebody else,
To have made a small difference simply being myself,
To believe this three-ringed circus
Has fulfilled some earthly purpose.

I want to matter
Before I am gone,
To have once been the shoulder that someone leaned on,
To have been the safe harbor in someone's sad storm,
To know someone was blessed because I was born.

I want to matter
As much as I'm able,
To be more than a faded face framed on some table.
For if I'm to be framed, I want it to be
In somebody's heart for eternity.

Though I'm fragile and foolish and flawed, I'm sincere.
I want someone to fondly remember me here.

More than being praised, more than being flattered,
I need to know without a doubt that somehow I have mattered.

And if I'm really honest,
I would like to write one song
That someone will be singing long after I am gone.

Acknowledgments

As with any goal in one's life, no one accomplishes it all alone. I'm grateful to so many who contributed to birthing this baby. First of all, my friend Matt Baugher, who initially suggested the book and gave it its name and proceeded to convince me he was a genius. I love you, Matt, and you are.

And to Theresa Peters and Albert Lee from UTA for believing in it and making it actually happen.

Thanks also to Debbie Wickwire for her unerring ability to get "to the point" but maintain the heart in the editing process. She knows I hate it, but she also knows I love her, so somehow we got through it.

Much love and thanks to Jeremy Cowart, Melissa Luther, and Rebekah Alonso for making the cover art come to light and life.

And, as always, to my dearest friend, Christine Gardner, who has the unenviable job of trying to keep me focused and finish the book. I love you, Chrissie. You are priceless.

And, finally, of course to my children, Cody and Cassidy, who never let me forget for a moment how human I am. But how much they love me anyway.

I'm sure there are others, but I'm old now and I can't remember who they are.

Notes

1. Lawrence K. Altman, "Deaths from AIDs Decline Sharply in New York City," *New York Times*, January 25, 1997, https://www.nytimes.com /1997/01/25/nyregion/deaths-from-aids-decline-sharply-in-new-york -city.html.
2. These lyrics eventually appeared in the song "Stand Up!" from the Broadway musical *Scandalous*.
3. Michael M. Homan, "Did the Ancient Israelites Drink Beer?," *Biblical Archaeology Review* 35, no. 5 (September/October 2010): https://www .baslibrary.org/biblical-archaeology-review/36/5/4.
4. Billy Graham, Congressional Gold Medal acceptance speech, United States Capitol, May 2, 1996, Washington, DC, C-Span video, 53:09, https://www.c-span.org/video/?71572–1/congressional-gold-medal.